Connected Mathematics 2™

P9-BZG-288

Moving Straight Ahead

Linear Relationships

Glenda Lappan
James T. Fey
William M. Fitzgerald
Susan N. Friel
Elizabeth Difanis Phillips

PEARSON
Prentice Hall

Boston, Massachusetts
Upper Saddle River, New Jersey

Connected Mathematics™ was developed at Michigan State University with financial support from the Michigan State University Office of the Provost, Computing and Technology, and the College of Natural Science.

This material is based upon work supported by the National Science Foundation under Grant No. MDR 9150217 and Grant No. ESI 9986372. Opinions expressed are those of the authors and not necessarily those of the Foundation.

The Michigan State University authors and administration have agreed that all MSU royalties arising from this publication will be devoted to purposes supported by the MSU Mathematics Education Enrichment Fund.

Acknowledgments appear on page 103, which constitutes an extension of this copyright page.

ISBN 0-13-165642-2
4 5 6 7 8 9 10   09 08 07 06

Authors of Connected Mathematics

(from left to right) Glenda Lappan, Betty Phillips, Susan Friel, Bill Fitzgerald, Jim Fey

Glenda Lappan is a University Distinguished Professor in the Department of Mathematics at Michigan State University. Her research and development interests are in the connected areas of students' learning of mathematics and mathematics teachers' professional growth and change related to the development and enactment of K–12 curriculum materials.

James T. Fey is a Professor of Curriculum and Instruction and Mathematics at the University of Maryland. His consistent professional interest has been development and research focused on curriculum materials that engage middle and high school students in problem-based collaborative investigations of mathematical ideas and their applications.

William M. Fitzgerald *(Deceased)* was a Professor in the Department of Mathematics at Michigan State University. His early research was on the use of concrete materials in supporting student learning and led to the development of teaching materials for laboratory environments. Later he helped develop a teaching model to support student experimentation with mathematics.

Susan N. Friel is a Professor of Mathematics Education in the School of Education at the University of North Carolina at Chapel Hill. Her research interests focus on statistics education for middle-grade students and, more broadly, on teachers' professional development and growth in teaching mathematics K–8.

Elizabeth Difanis Phillips is a Senior Academic Specialist in the Mathematics Department of Michigan State University. She is interested in teaching and learning mathematics for both teachers and students. These interests have led to curriculum and professional development projects at the middle school and high school levels, as well as projects related to the teaching and learning of algebra across the grades.

CMP2 Development Staff

Field Test Sites for CMP2

During the development of the revised edition of *Connected Mathematics* (CMP2), more than 100 classroom teachers have field-tested materials at 49 school sites in 12 states and the District of Columbia. This classroom testing occurred over three academic years (2001 through 2004), allowing careful study of the effectiveness of each of the 24 units that comprise the program. A special thanks to the students and teachers at these pilot schools.

Arkansas

Magnolia Public Schools
Kittena Bell*, Judith Trowell*; *Central Elementary School:* Maxine Broom, Betty Eddy, Tiffany Fallin, Bonnie Flurry, Carolyn Monk, Elizabeth Tye; *Magnolia Junior High School:* Monique Bryan, Ginger Cook, David Graham, Shelby Lamkin

Colorado

Boulder Public Schools
Nevin Platt Middle School: Judith Koenig

St. Vrain Valley School District, Longmont
Westview Middle School: Colleen Beyer, Kitty Canupp, Ellie Decker*, Peggy McCarthy, Tanya deNobrega, Cindy Payne, Ericka Pilon, Andrew Roberts

District of Columbia

Capitol Hill Day School: Ann Lawrence

Georgia

University of Georgia, Athens
Brad Findell

Madison Public Schools
Morgan County Middle School: Renee Burgdorf, Lynn Harris, Nancy Kurtz, Carolyn Stewart

Maine

Falmouth Public Schools
Falmouth Middle School: Donna Erikson, Joyce Hebert, Paula Hodgkins, Rick Hogan, David Legere, Cynthia Martin, Barbara Stiles, Shawn Towle*

Michigan

Portland Public Schools
Portland Middle School: Mark Braun, Holly DeRosia, Kathy Dole*, Angie Foote, Teri Keusch, Tammi Wardwell

Traverse City Area Public Schools
Bertha Vos Elementary: Kristin Sak; *Central Grade School:* Michelle Clark; Jody Meyers; *Eastern Elementary:* Karrie Tufts; *Interlochen Elementary:* Mary McGee-Cullen; *Long Lake Elementary:* Julie Faulkner*, Charlie Maxbauer, Katherine Sleder; *Norris Elementary:* Hope Slanaker; *Oak Park Elementary:* Jessica Steed; *Traverse Heights Elementary:* Jennifer Wolfert; *Westwoods Elementary:* Nancy Conn; *Old Mission Peninsula School:* Deb Larimer; *Traverse City East Junior High:* Ivanka Berkshire, Ruthanne Kladder, Jan Palkowski, Jane Peterson, Mary Beth Schmitt; *Traverse City West Junior High:* Dan Fouch*, Ray Fouch

Sturgis Public Schools
Sturgis Middle School: Ellen Eisele

Minnesota

Burnsville School District 191
Hidden Valley Elementary: Stephanie Cin, Jane McDevitt

Hopkins School District 270
Alice Smith Elementary: Sandra Cowing, Kathleen Gustafson, Martha Mason, Scott Stillman; *Eisenhower Elementary:* Chad Bellig, Patrick Berger, Nancy Glades, Kye Johnson, Shane Wasserman, Victoria Wilson; *Gatewood Elementary:* Sarah Ham, Julie Kloos, Janine Pung, Larry Wade; *Glen Lake Elementary:* Jacqueline Cramer, Kathy Hering, Cecelia Morris, Robb Trenda; *Katherine Curren Elementary:* Diane Bancroft, Sue DeWit, John Wilson; *L. H. Tanglen Elementary:* Kevin Athmann, Lisa Becker, Mary LaBelle, Kathy Rezac, Roberta Severson; *Meadowbrook Elementary:* Jan Gauger, Hildy Shank, Jessica Zimmerman; *North Junior High:* Laurel Hahn, Kristin Lee, Jodi Markuson, Bruce Mestemacher, Laurel Miller, Bonnie Rinker, Jeannine Salzer, Sarah Shafer, Cam Stottler; *West Junior High:* Alicia Beebe, Kristie Earl, Nobu Fujii, Pam Georgetti, Susan Gilbert, Regina Nelson Johnson, Debra Lindstrom, Michele Luke*, Jon Sorenson

Minneapolis School District 1
Ann Sullivan K-8 School: Bronwyn Collins; Anne Bartel* (Curriculum and Instruction Office)

Wayzata School District 284
Central Middle School: Sarajane Myers, Dan Nielsen, Tanya Ravenholdt

White Bear Lake School District 624
Central Middle School: Amy Jorgenson, Michelle Reich, Brenda Sammon

New York

New York City Public Schools
IS 89: Yelena Aynbinder, Chi-Man Ng, Nina Rapaport, Joel Spengler, Phyllis Tam*, Brent Wyso; *Wagner Middle School:* Jason Appel, Intissar Fernandez, Yee Gee Get, Richard Goldstein, Irving Marcus, Sue Norton, Bernadita Owens, Jennifer Rehn*, Kevin Yuhas

---

* indicates a Field Test Site Coordinator

Ohio

Talawanda School District, Oxford
Talawanda Middle School: Teresa Abrams, Larry Brock, Heather Brosey, Julie Churchman, Monna Even, Karen Fitch, Bob George, Amanda Klee, Pat Meade, Sandy Montgomery, Barbara Sherman, Lauren Steidl

Miami University
Jeffrey Wanko*

Springfield Public Schools
Rockway School: Jim Mamer

Pennsylvania

Pittsburgh Public Schools
Kenneth Labuskes, Marianne O'Connor, Mary Lynn Raith*; *Arthur J. Rooney Middle School:* David Hairston, Stamatina Mousetis, Alfredo Zangaro; *Frick International Studies Academy:* Suzanne Berry, Janet Falkowski, Constance Finseth, Romika Hodge, Frank Machi; *Reizenstein Middle School:* Jeff Baldwin, James Brautigam, Lorena Burnett, Glen Cobbett, Michael Jordan, Margaret Lazur, Melissa Munnell, Holly Neely, Ingrid Reed, Dennis Reft

Texas

Austin Independent School District
Bedichek Middle School: Lisa Brown, Jennifer Glasscock, Vicki Massey

El Paso Independent School District
Cordova Middle School: Armando Aguirre, Anneliesa Durkes, Sylvia Guzman, Pat Holguin*, William Holguin, Nancy Nava, Laura Orozco, Michelle Peña, Roberta Rosen, Patsy Smith, Jeremy Wolf

Plano Independent School District
Patt Henry, James Wohlgehagen*; *Frankford Middle School:* Mandy Baker, Cheryl Butsch, Amy Dudley, Betsy Eshelman, Janet Greene, Cort Haynes, Kathy Letchworth, Kay Marshall, Kelly McCants, Amy Reck, Judy Scott, Syndy Snyder, Lisa Wang; *Wilson Middle School:* Darcie Bane, Amanda Bedenko, Whitney Evans, Tonelli Hatley, Sarah (Becky) Higgs, Kelly Johnston, Rebecca McElligott, Kay Neuse, Cheri Slocum, Kelli Straight

Washington

Evergreen School District
Shahala Middle School: Nicole Abrahamsen, Terry Coon*, Carey Doyle, Sheryl Drechsler, George Gemma, Gina Helland, Amy Hilario, Darla Lidyard, Sean McCarthy, Tilly Meyer, Willow Neuwelt, Todd Parsons, Brian Pederson, Stan Posey, Shawn Scott, Craig Sjoberg, Lynette Sundstrom, Charles Switzer, Luke Youngblood

Wisconsin

Beaver Dam Unified School District
Beaver Dam Middle School: Jim Braemer, Jeanne Frick, Jessica Greatens, Barbara Link, Dennis McCormick, Karen Michels, Nancy Nichols*, Nancy Palm, Shelly Stelsel, Susan Wiggins

* indicates a Field Test Site Coordinator

Reviews of CMP to Guide Development of CMP2

Before writing for CMP2 began or field tests were conducted, the first edition of *Connected Mathematics* was submitted to the mathematics faculties of school districts from many parts of the country and to 80 individual reviewers for extensive comments.

School District Survey Reviews of CMP

Arizona
Madison School District #38 (Phoenix)

Arkansas
Cabot School District, Little Rock School District, Magnolia School District

California
Los Angeles Unified School District

Colorado
St. Vrain Valley School District (Longmont)

Florida
Leon County Schools (Tallahassee)

Illinois
School District #21 (Wheeling)

Indiana
Joseph L. Block Junior High (East Chicago)

Kentucky
Fayette County Public Schools (Lexington)

Maine
Selection of Schools

Massachusetts
Selection of Schools

Michigan
Sparta Area Schools

Minnesota
Hopkins School District

Texas
Austin Independent School District, The El Paso Collaborative for Academic Excellence, Plano Independent School District

Wisconsin
Platteville Middle School

Individual Reviewers of CMP

Arkansas
Deborah Cramer; Robby Frizzell *(Taylor)*; Lowell Lynde *(University of Arkansas, Monticello)*; Leigh Manzer *(Norfork)*; Lynne Roberts *(Emerson High School, Emerson)*; Tony Timms *(Cabot Public Schools)*; Judith Trowell *(Arkansas Department of Higher Education)*

California
José Alcantar *(Gilroy)*; Eugenie Belcher *(Gilroy)*; Marian Pasternack *(Lowman M. S. T. Center, North Hollywood)*; Susana Pezoa *(San Jose)*; Todd Rabusin *(Hollister)*; Margaret Siegfried *(Ocala Middle School, San Jose)*; Polly Underwood *(Ocala Middle School, San Jose)*

Colorado
Janeane Golliher *(St. Vrain Valley School District, Longmont)*; Judith Koenig *(Nevin Platt Middle School, Boulder)*

Florida
Paige Loggins *(Swift Creek Middle School, Tallahassee)*

Illinois
Jan Robinson *(School District #21, Wheeling)*

Indiana
Frances Jackson *(Joseph L. Block Junior High, East Chicago)*

Kentucky
Natalee Feese *(Fayette County Public Schools, Lexington)*

Maine
Betsy Berry *(Maine Math & Science Alliance, Augusta)*

Maryland
Joseph Gagnon *(University of Maryland, College Park)*; Paula Maccini *(University of Maryland, College Park)*

Massachusetts
George Cobb *(Mt. Holyoke College, South Hadley)*; Cliff Kanold *(University of Massachusetts, Amherst)*

Michigan
Mary Bouck *(Farwell Area Schools)*; Carol Dorer *(Slauson Middle School, Ann Arbor)*; Carrie Heaney *(Forsythe Middle School, Ann Arbor)*; Ellen Hopkins *(Clague Middle School, Ann Arbor)*; Teri Keusch *(Portland Middle School, Portland)*; Valerie Mills *(Oakland Schools, Waterford)*; Mary Beth Schmitt *(Traverse City East Junior High, Traverse City)*; Jack Smith *(Michigan State University, East Lansing)*; Rebecca Spencer *(Sparta Middle School, Sparta)*; Ann Marie Nicoll Turner *(Tappan Middle School, Ann Arbor)*; Scott Turner *(Scarlett Middle School, Ann Arbor)*

Minnesota
Margarita Alvarez *(Olson Middle School, Minneapolis)*; Jane Amundson *(Nicollet Junior High, Burnsville)*; Anne Bartel *(Minneapolis Public Schools)*; Gwen Ranzau Campbell *(Sunrise Park Middle School, White Bear Lake)*; Stephanie Cin *(Hidden Valley Elementary, Burnsville)*; Joan Garfield *(University of Minnesota, Minneapolis)*; Gretchen Hall *(Richfield Middle School, Richfield)*; Jennifer Larson *(Olson Middle School, Minneapolis)*; Michele Luke *(West Junior High, Minnetonka)*; Jeni Meyer *(Richfield Junior High, Richfield)*; Judy Pfingsten *(Inver Grove Heights Middle School, Inver Grove Heights)*; Sarah Shafer *(North Junior High, Minnetonka)*; Genni Steele *(Central Middle School, White Bear Lake)*; Victoria Wilson *(Eisenhower Elementary, Hopkins)*; Paul Zorn *(St. Olaf College, Northfield)*

New York
Debra Altenau-Bartolino *(Greenwich Village Middle School, New York)*; Doug Clements *(University of Buffalo)*; Francis Curcio *(New York University, New York)*; Christine Dorosh *(Clinton School for Writers, Brooklyn)*; Jennifer Rehn *(East Side Middle School, New York)*; Phyllis Tam *(IS 89 Lab School, New York)*;

Marie Turini *(Louis Armstrong Middle School, New York)*; Lucy West *(Community School District 2, New York)*; Monica Witt *(Simon Baruch Intermediate School 104, New York)*

Pennsylvania
Robert Aglietti *(Pittsburgh)*; Sharon Mihalich *(Pittsburgh)*; Jennifer Plumb *(South Hills Middle School, Pittsburgh)*; Mary Lynn Raith *(Pittsburgh Public Schools)*

Texas
Michelle Bittick *(Austin Independent School District)*; Margaret Cregg *(Plano Independent School District)*; Sheila Cunningham *(Klein Independent School District)*; Judy Hill *(Austin Independent School District)*; Patricia Holguin *(El Paso Independent School District)*; Bonnie McNemar *(Arlington)*; Kay Neuse *(Plano Independent School District)*; Joyce Polanco *(Austin Independent School District)*; Marge Ramirez *(University of Texas at El Paso)*; Pat Rossman *(Baker Campus, Austin)*; Cindy Schimek *(Houston)*; Cynthia Schneider *(Charles A. Dana Center, University of Texas at Austin)*; Uri Treisman *(Charles A. Dana Center, University of Texas at Austin)*; Jacqueline Weilmuenster *(Grapevine-Colleyville Independent School District)*; LuAnn Weynand *(San Antonio)*; Carmen Whitman *(Austin Independent School District)*; James Wohlgehagen *(Plano Independent School District)*

Washington
Ramesh Gangolli *(University of Washington, Seattle)*

Wisconsin
Susan Lamon *(Marquette University, Hales Corner)*; Steve Reinhart *(retired, Chippewa Falls Middle School, Eau Claire)*

Table of Contents

Moving Straight Ahead
Linear Relationships

Unit Opener 2

Mathematical Highlights 4

Investigation 1 Walking Rates 5

    1.1 Walking Marathons: Finding and Using Rates 5

    1.2 Walking Rates and Linear Relationships: Linear Relationships in
        Tables, Graphs, and Equations 6

    1.3 Raising Money: Using Linear Relationships 8

    1.4 Using the Walkathon Money: Recognizing Linear Relationships 10

    ACE Homework 12

    Mathematical Reflections 23

**Investigation 2 Exploring Linear Functions
With Graphs and Tables** 24

    2.1 Walking to Win: Finding the Point of Intersection 24

    2.2 Crossing the Line: Using Tables, Graphs, and Equations 25

    2.3 Comparing Costs: Comparing Equations 27

    2.4 Connecting Tables, Graphs, and Equations 29

    ACE Homework 31

    Mathematical Reflections 45

Investigation 3 Solving Equations **46**

3.1 Solving Equations Using Tables and Graphs **47**

3.2 Exploring Equality **48**

3.3 From Pouches to Variables: Writing Equations **51**

3.4 Solving Linear Equations **53**

3.5 Finding the Point of Intersection **55**

ACE Homework **57**

Mathematical Reflections **69**

Investigation 4 Exploring Slope **70**

4.1 Climbing Stairs: Using Rise and Run **70**

4.2 Finding the Slope of a Line **72**

4.3 Exploring Patterns With Lines **75**

4.4 Pulling It All Together: Writing Equations With Two Variables **76**

ACE Homework **78**

Mathematical Reflections **89**

The Unit Project: Conducting an Experiment **90**

Looking Back and Looking Ahead **94**

English/Spanish Glossary **97**

Index **101**

Acknowledgments **103**

Moving Straight Ahead

Linear Relationships

Henri challenges his older brother Emile to a walking race. Emile walks 2.5 meters per second, and Henri walks 1 meter per second. Emile gives Henri a 45-meter head start. What distance wll allow Henri to win in a close race?

You can estimate the temperature outside by counting cricket chirps. Suppose a cricket chirps n times in one minute. The temperature t in degrees Fahrenheit can be computed with the formula $t = \frac{1}{4}n + 40$. What is the temperature if a cricket chirps 150 times in a minute?

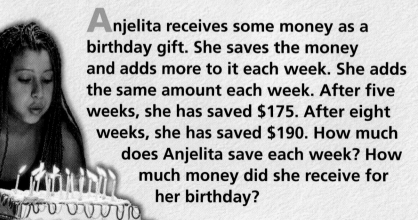

Anjelita receives some money as a birthday gift. She saves the money and adds more to it each week. She adds the same amount each week. After five weeks, she has saved $175. After eight weeks, she has saved $190. How much does Anjelita save each week? How much money did she receive for her birthday?

All around you, things occur in patterns. Once you observe a pattern, you can use the pattern to predict information beyond and between the data observed. The ability to use patterns to make predictions makes it possible for a baseball player to run to the right position to catch a fly ball or for a pilot to estimate the flying time for a trip.

In *Variables and Patterns*, you investigated relationships between variables. The relationships were displayed as tables, graphs, and equations. Some of the graphs, such as the graph of distance and time for a van traveling at a steady rate, were straight lines. Relationships with graphs that are straight lines are called *linear relationships*.

In this unit, you will study linear relationships. You will learn about the characteristics of a linear relationship and how to determine whether a relationship is linear by looking at its equation or at a table of values. You will use what you learn about linear relationships to answer questions like those on the facing page.

Mathematical Highlights

Linear Relationships

In *Moving Straight Ahead*, you will explore properties of linearity.

You will learn how to

- Recognize problem situations in which two or more variables have a linear relationship to each other
- Construct tables, graphs, and symbolic equations that express linear relationships
- Translate information about linear relations given in a table, a graph, or an equation to one of the other forms
- Understand the connections between linear equations and the patterns in the tables and graphs of those equations: rate of change, slope, and *y*-intercept
- Solve linear equations
- Solve problems and make decisions about linear relationships using information given in tables, graphs, and symbolic expressions
- Use tables, graphs, and equations of linear relations to answer questions

As you work on the problems in this unit, ask yourself questions about problem situations that involve related quantities:

What are the variables in the problem?

Do the variables in this problem have a linear relationship to each other?

What patterns in the problem suggest that it is linear?

How can the linear relationship be represented in a problem, in a table, in a graph, or with an equation?

How do changes in one variable affect changes in a related variable?

How are these changes captured in a table, graph, or equation?

How can tables, graphs, and equations of linear relationships be used to answer questions?

Investigation 1

Walking Rates

In *Variables and Patterns*, you read about a bicycle touring business. You used tables, graphs, and equations to represent patterns relating variables such as cost, income, and profit. You looked at some linear relationships, like the relationship between cost and number of rental bikes represented in this graph:

Relationships that are represented by straight lines on a graph are called **linear relationships** or **linear functions.** From the graph, you see that the relationship between the number of bikes rented and the total rental cost is a linear function. In this investigation, you will consider the questions:

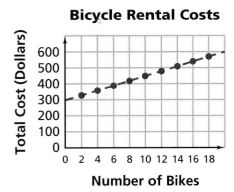

Bicycle Rental Costs

How can you determine whether a relationship is linear by examining a table of data or an equation?

How do changes in one variable affect changes in a related variable? How are these changes captured in a table, a graph, or an equation?

1.1 Walking Marathons

Ms. Chang's class decides to participate in a walkathon. Each participant must find sponsors to pledge a certain amount of money for each kilometer the participant walks. Leanne suggests that they determine their walking rates in meters per second so they can make predictions.

Do you know what your walking rate is?

Problem 1.1 Finding and Using Rates

To determine your walking rate:

- Line up ten meter sticks, end to end (or mark off 10 meters), in the hall of your school.
- Have a partner time your walk.
- Start at one end and walk the length of the ten meter sticks using your normal walking pace.

A. What is your walking rate in meters per second?

B. Assume you continue to walk at this constant rate.

    1. How long would it take you to walk 500 meters?

    2. How far could you walk in 30 seconds? In 10 minutes? In 1 hour?

    3. Describe in words the distance in meters you could walk in a given number of seconds.

    4. Write an equation that represents the distance d in meters that you could walk in t seconds if you maintain this pace.

    5. Use the equation to predict the distance you would walk in 45 seconds.

ACE Homework starts on page 12.

1.2 Walking Rates and Linear Relationships

Think about the effect a walking rate has on the relationship between time walked and distance walked. This will provide some important clues about how to identify linear relationships from tables, graphs, and equations.

Problem 1.2 Linear Relationships in Tables, Graphs, and Equations

Here are the walking rates that Gilberto, Alana, and Leanne found in their experiment.

Name	Walking Rate
Alana	1 meter per second
Gilberto	2 meters per second
Leanne	2.5 meters per second

A. 1. Make a table showing the distance walked by each student for the first ten seconds. How does the walking rate affect the data?

  2. Graph the time and distance on the same coordinate axes. Use a different color for each student's data. How does the walking rate affect the graph?

  3. Write an equation that gives the relationship between the time *t* and the distance *d* walked for each student. How is the walking rate represented in the equations?

B. For each student:

  1. If *t* increases by 1 second, by how much does the distance change? How is this change represented in a table? In a graph?

  2. If *t* increases by 5 seconds, by how much does the distance change? How is this change represented in a table? In a graph?

  3. What is the walking rate per minute? The walking rate per hour?

C. Four other friends who are part of the walkathon made the following representations of their data. Are any of these relationships linear relationships? Explain.

George's Walking Rate	
Time (seconds)	Distance (meters)
0	0
1	2
2	9
3	11
4	20
5	25

Elizabeth's Walking Rate	
Time (seconds)	Distance (meters)
0	0
2	3
4	6
6	9
8	12
10	15

Billie's Walking Rate
$$D = 2.25t$$

D represents distance
t represents time

Bob's Walking Rate
$$t = \frac{100}{r}$$

t represents time
r represents walking rate

ACE **Homework starts on page 12.**

1.3 Raising Money

In *Variables and Patterns*, you looked at situations that involved *dependent* and *independent variables*. Because the distance walked depends on the time, you know distance is the dependent variable and time is the independent variable. In this problem, you will look at relationships between two other variables in a walkathon.

Getting Ready for Problem

Each participant in the walkathon must find sponsors to pledge a certain amount of money for each kilometer the participant walks.

The students in Ms. Chang's class are trying to estimate how much money they might be able to raise. Several questions come up in their discussions:

- What variables can affect the amount of money that is collected?
- How can you use these variables to estimate the amount of money each student will collect?
- Will the amount of money collected be the same for each walker? Explain.

Each student found sponsors who are willing to pledge the following amounts.

- Leanne's sponsors will pay $10 regardless of how far she walks.
- Gilberto's sponsors will pay $2 per kilometer (km).
- Alana's sponsors will make a $5 donation plus 50¢ per kilometer.

The class refers to these as *pledge plans*.

Problem 1.3 Using Linear Relationships

active math online

For: Climbing Monkeys Activity
Visit: PHSchool.com
Web Code: and-5103

A. 1. Make a table for each student's pledge plan, showing the amount of money each of his or her sponsors would owe if he or she walked distances from 0 to 6 kilometers. What are the dependent and independent variables?

2. Graph the three pledge plans on the same coordinate axes. Use a different color for each plan.

3. Write an equation for each pledge plan. Explain what information each number and variable in your equation represents.

4. a. What pattern of change for each pledge plan do you observe in the table?

b. How does this pattern appear in the graph? In the equation?

B. 1. Suppose each student walks 8 kilometers in the walkathon. How much money does each sponsor owe?

2. Suppose each student receives $10 from a sponsor. How many kilometers does each student walk?

3. On which graph does the point (12, 11) lie? What information does this point represent?

4. In Alana's plan, how is the fixed $5 donation represented in

a. the table? **b.** the graph? **c.** the equation?

C. Gilberto decides to give a T-shirt to each of his sponsors. Each shirt costs him $4.75. He plans to pay for each shirt with some of the money he collects from each sponsor.

1. Write an equation that represents the amount of money Gilberto makes from each sponsor after he has paid for the T-shirts. Explain what information each number and variable in the equation represents.

2. Graph the equation for distances from 0 to 5 kilometers.

3. Compare this graph to the graph of Gilberto's pledge plan in Question A, part (2).

ACE Homework starts on page 12.

1.4 Using the Walkathon Money

Ms. Chang's class decides to use their money from the walkathon to provide books for the children's ward at the hospital. They put the money in the school safe and withdraw a fixed amount each week to buy new books. To keep track of the money, Isabella makes a table of the amount of money in the account at the end of each week.

Week	Amount of Money at the End of Each Week
0	$144
1	$132
2	$120
3	$108
4	$96
5	$84

What do you think the graph would look like?

Is this a linear relationship?

Problem 1.4 Recognizing Linear Relationships

A. 1. How much money is in the account at the start of the project?

2. How much money is withdrawn from the account each week?

3. Is the relationship between the number of weeks and the amount of money left in the account a linear relationship? Explain.

4. Suppose the students continue withdrawing the same amount of money each week. Sketch a graph of this relationship.

5. Write an equation that represents the relationship. Explain what information each number and variable represents.

B. Mr. Mamer's class also raised money from the walkathon. They use their money to buy games and puzzles for the children's ward. Sade uses a graph to keep track of the amount of money in their account at the end of each week.

Money in Mr. Mamer's Class Account

1. What information does the graph represent about the money in Mr. Mamer's class account?

2. Make a table of data for the first 10 weeks. Explain why the table represents a linear relationship.

3. Write an equation that represents the linear relationship. Explain what information each number and variable represents.

C. How can you determine if a relationship is linear from a graph, table, or equation?

D. Compare the linear relationships in this problem with those in previous problems in this investigation.

ACE Homework starts on page 12.

Applications

1. Hoshi walks 10 meters in 3 seconds.

   a. What is her walking rate?

   b. At this rate, how long does it take her to walk 100 meters?

   c. Suppose she walks this same rate for 50 seconds. How far does she walk?

   d. Write an equation that represents the distance d that Hoshi walks in t seconds.

2. Milo walks 40 meters in 15 seconds and Mira walks 30 meters in 10 seconds. Whose walking rate is faster?

In Exercises 3–5, Jose, Mario, Melanie, Mike, and Alicia are on a weeklong cycling trip. Cycling times include only biking time, not time to eat, rest, and so on.

3. The table below gives the distance Jose, Mario, and Melanie travel for the first 3 hours. Assume that each person cycles at a constant rate.

Cycling Distance

Cycling Time (hours)	Distance (miles)		
	Jose	Mario	Melanie
0	0	0	0
1	5	7	9
2	10	14	18
3	15	21	27

   a. Find the average rate at which each person travels during the first 3 hours. Explain.

   b. Find the distance each person travels in 7 hours.

   c. Graph the time and distance data for all three riders on the same coordinate axes.

   d. Use the graphs to find the distance each person travels in $6\frac{1}{2}$ hours.

   e. Use the graphs to find the time it takes each person to travel 70 miles.

f. How does the rate at which each person rides affect each graph?

g. For each rider, write an equation that can be used to calculate the distance traveled after a given number of hours.

h. Use your equations from part (g) to calculate the distance each person travels in $6\frac{1}{2}$ hours.

i. How does a person's biking rate show up in his or her equation?

4. Mike makes the following table of the distances he travels during the first day of the trip.

Cycling Distance

Time (hours)	Distance (miles)
0	0
1	6.5
2	13
3	19.5
4	26
5	32.5
6	39

a. Suppose Mike continues riding at this rate. Write an equation for the distance Mike travels after t hours.

b. Sketch a graph of the equation. How did you choose the range of values for the time axis? For the distance axis?

c. How can you find the distances Mike travels in 7 hours and in $9\frac{1}{2}$ hours, using the table? Using the graph? Using the equation?

d. How can you find the numbers of hours it takes Mike to travel 100 miles and 237 miles, using the table? Using the graph? Using the equation?

e. For parts (c) and (d), what are the advantages and disadvantages of using each form of representation—a table, a graph, and an equation—to find the answers?

f. Compare the rate at which Mike rides with the rates at which Jose, Mario, and Melanie ride. Who rides the fastest? How can you determine this from the tables? From the graphs? From the equations?

5. The distance Alicia travels in t hours is represented by the equation $d = 7.5t$.

   a. At what rate does Alicia travel?

   b. Suppose the graph of Alicia's distance and time is put on the same set of axes as Mike's, Jose's, Mario's, and Melanie's graphs. Where would it be located in relationship to each of the graphs? Describe the location without actually making the graph.

6. The graph below represents the walkathon pledge plans from three sponsors.

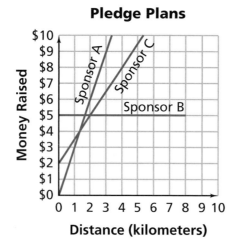

Pledge Plans

   a. Describe each sponsor's pledge plan.

   b. What is the number of dollars per kilometer each sponsor pledges?

   c. What does the point where the line crosses the y-axis mean for each sponsor?

   d. Write the coordinates of two points on each line. What information does each point represent for the sponsor's pledge plan?

7. The students in Ms. Chang's class decide to order water bottles that advertise the walkathon. Maliik obtains two different quotes for the costs of the bottles.

     Fill It Up charges $4 per bottle.

     Bottles by Bob charges $25 plus $3 per bottle.

   a. For each company, write an equation Maliik could use to calculate the cost for any number of bottles.

b. On the same set of axes, graph both equations from part (a). Which variable is the independent variable? Which is the dependent variable?

c. Which company do you think the class should buy water bottles from? What factors influenced your decision?

d. For what number of water bottles is the cost the same for both companies?

8. Multiple Choice The equation $C = 5n$ represents the cost C in dollars for n caps that advertise the walkathon. Which of the following pairs of numbers could represent a number of caps and the cost for that number of caps, (n, C)?

A. $(0, 5)$ **B.** $(3, 15)$ **C.** $(15, 60)$ **D.** $(5, 1)$

9. The equation $d = 3.5t + 50$ represents the distance d in meters that a cyclist is from his home after t seconds.

Homework
Help **O**nline
PHSchool.com
For: Help with Exercise 9
Web Code: ane-5109

a. Which of the following pairs of numbers represent the coordinates of a point on the graph of this equation? Explain your answer.

  i. $(10, 85)$ **ii.** $(0, 0)$ **iii.** $(3, 60.5)$

b. What information do the coordinates represent about the cyclist?

10. Examine the patterns in each table.

Table 1			Table 2			Table 3			Table 4	
x	**y**		**x**	**y**		**x**	**y**		**x**	**y**
−2	3		−3	9		0	10		0	−3
−1	3		−2	4		3	19		2	−6
0	3		−1	1		5	25		4	−9
1	3		0	0		10	40		6	−12
2	3		1	1		12	46		8	−15

a. Describe the similarities and differences in Tables 1–4.

b. Explain how you can use the tables to decide if the data represent a linear relationship.

c. Sketch a graph of the data in each table.

d. Write an equation for each linear relationship. Explain what information the numbers and variables represent in the relationship.

11. The temperature at the North Pole is 30°F and is expected to drop 5°F per hour for the next several hours. Write an equation that represents the relationship between temperature and time. Explain what information your numbers and variables mean. Is this a linear relationship?

12. Jamal's parents give him money to spend at camp. Jamal spends the same amount of money on snacks each day. The table below shows the amount of money, in dollars, he has left at the end of each day.

Snack Money

Days	Money Left
0	$20
1	$18
2	$16
3	$14
4	$12
5	$10
6	$8

a. How much money does Jamal have at the start of camp? Explain.

b. How much money is spent each day? Explain.

c. Assume that Jamal's spending pattern continues. Is the relationship between the number of days and the amount of money left in Jamal's wallet a linear relationship? Explain.

d. Check your answer to part (c) by sketching a graph of this relationship.

e. Write an equation that represents the relationship. Explain what information the numbers and variables represent.

13. Write an equation for each graph.

Go Online
PHSchool.com

For: Multiple-Choice Skills Practice
Web Code: ana-5154

Graph 1   **Graph 2**

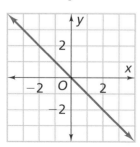   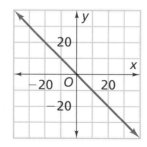

14. a. Give an example of a linear situation with a rate of change that is

   i. positive.   **ii.** zero (no change).   **iii.** negative.

   b. Write an equation that represents each situation in part (a).

Connections

15. Jelani is in a walking race at his school. In the first 20 seconds, he walks 60 meters. In the next 30 seconds, he walks 60 meters. In the next 10 seconds, he walks 35 meters. In the last 40 seconds, he walks 80 meters.

   a. Describe how Jelani's walking rate changes during the race.

   b. What would a graph of Jelani's walking race look like?

16. Insert parentheses where needed in each expression to show how to get each result.

   a. $2 + -3 \times 4 = -10$

   b. $4 + -3 \times -4 = -4$

   c. $-12 \div 2 + -4 = 6$

   d. $8 \div -2 + -2 = -6$

17. Which of the following number sentences are true? In each case, explain how you could answer without any calculation. Check your answers by doing the indicated calculations.

   a. $20 \times 410 = (20 \times 400) + (20 \times 10)$

   b. $20 \times 308 = (20 \times 340) - (20 \times 32)$

   c. $-20 \times -800 = (-20 \times -1{,}000) + (-20 \times 200)$

   d. $-20 + (300 \times 32) = (-20 + 300) \times (-20 + 32)$

18. Fill in the missing numbers to make each sentence true.

   a. $15 \times (6 + 4) = (15 \times \blacksquare) + (15 \times 4)$

   b. $2 \times (x + 6) = (2 \times \blacksquare) + (\blacksquare \times 6)$

   c. $(x \times 2) + (x \times 6) = \blacksquare \times (2 + 6)$

19. a. Draw a rectangle whose area can be represented by the expression $5 \times (12 + 6)$.

   b. Write another expression to represent the area of the rectangle in part (a).

20. Find the unit rate and use it to write an equation relating the two quantities.

   a. 50 dollars for 150 T-shirts

   b. 8 dollars to rent 14 video games

   c. 24 tablespoons of sugar in 3 glasses of Bolda Cola

21. The longest human-powered sporting event is the Tour de France cycling race. The record average speed for this race is 25.88 miles per hour, which was attained by Lance Armstrong in 2005.

   a. The race was 2,242 miles long. How long did it take Armstrong to complete the race in 2005?

   b. Suppose Lance had reduced his average cycling rate by 0.1 mile per hour. By how much would his time have changed?

22. a. In 2002, Gillian O'Sullivan set the record of the 5,000 m race-walking event. She finished the race in 20 minutes 2.60 seconds. What was O'Sullivan's average walking speed, in meters per second?

   b. In 1990, Nadezhda Ryashkina set the record for the 10,000 m race-walking event. She finished this race in 41 minutes 56.23 seconds. What was Ryashkina's average walking rate, in meters per second?

23. A recipe for orange juice calls for 2 cups of orange juice concentrate and 3 cups of water. The table below shows the amount of concentrate and water needed to make a given number of batches of juice.

Orange Juice Mixture Amounts

Batches of Juice (b)	Concentrate (c)	Water (w)	Juice (j)
1	2 cups	3 cups	5 cups
2	4 cups	6 cups	10 cups
3	6 cups	9 cups	15 cups
4	8 cups	12 cups	20 cups

The relationship between the number of batches b of juice and the number of cups c of concentrate is linear. The equation for this relationship is $c = 2b$. Are there other linear relationships in this table? Sketch graphs or write equations for the linear relationships you find.

24. The table below gives information about a pineapple punch recipe. The table shows the number of cups of orange juice, pineapple juice, and soda water needed for different quantities of punch.

Recipe

J (orange juice, cups)	P (pineapple juice, cups)	S (soda water, cups)
1	▣	▣
2	▣	▣
3	▣	▣
4	12	6
5	▣	▣
6	▣	▣
7	▣	▣
8	24	12

The relationship between cups of orange juice and cups of pineapple juice is linear, and the relationship between cups of orange juice and cups of soda water is linear.

a. Zahara makes the recipe using 6 cups of orange juice. How many cups of soda water does she use? Explain your reasoning.

b. Patrick makes the recipe using 6 cups of pineapple juice. How many cups of orange juice and how many cups of soda water does he use? Explain.

25. The graph below represents the distance John runs in a race. Use the graph to describe John's progress during the course of the race. Does he run at a constant rate during the trip? Explain.

Running Distance

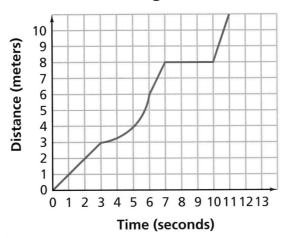

26. a. Does the graph represent a linear relationship? Explain.

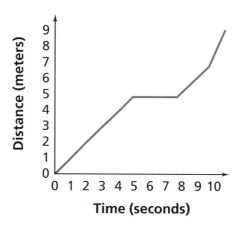

b. Could this graph represent a walking pattern? Explain.

In Exercises 27–29, students conduct an experiment to investigate the rate at which a leaking faucet loses water. They fill a paper cup with water, make a small hole in the bottom, and collect the dripping water in a measuring container, measuring the amount of water in the container at the end of each 10-second interval.

27. Students conducting the leaking-faucet experiment produce the table below. The measuring container they use holds only 100 milliliters.

a. Suppose the students continue their experiment. After how many seconds will the measuring container overflow?

Leaking Faucet

Time (seconds)	10	20	30	40	50	60	70
Water Loss (milliliters)	2	5	8.5	11.5	14	16.5	19.5

b. Is this relationship linear? Explain.

28. Denise and Takashi work together on the leaking-faucet experiment. Each of them makes a graph of the data they collect. What might have caused their graphs to look so different?

Denise's Graph   **Takashi's Graph**

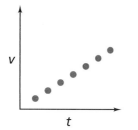   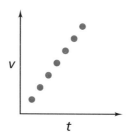

29. What information might the graph below represent in the leaking-faucet experiment?

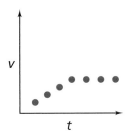

Extensions

30. a. The table below shows the population of four cities for the past eight years. Describe how the population of each city changed over the eight years.

Populations of Four Cities

Year	Population			
	Deep Valley	**Nowhere**	**Swampville**	**Mount Silicon**
0 (start)	1,000	1,000	1,000	1,000
1	1,500	900	1,500	2,000
2	2,000	800	2,500	4,000
3	2,500	750	3,000	8,000
4	3,000	700	5,000	16,000
5	3,500	725	3,000	32,000
6	4,000	900	2,500	64,000
7	4,500	1,500	1,500	128,000
8	5,000	1,700	1,000	256,000

b. Use the table to decide which relationships are linear.

c. Graph the data for each city. Describe how you selected ranges of values for the horizontal and vertical axes.

d. What are the advantages of using a table or a graph to represent the data?

31. In the walkathon, Jose decides to charge his patrons $10 for the first 5 kilometers he walks and $1 per kilometer after 5 kilometers.

    a. Sketch a graph that represents the relationship between money collected and kilometers walked.

    b. Compare this graph to the graphs of the other pledge plans in Problem 1.3.

32. The cost C to make T-shirts for the walkathon is represented by the equation $C = 20 + 5N$, where N is the number of T-shirts.

    a. Find the coordinates of a point that lies on the graph of this equation. Explain what the coordinates mean in this context.

    b. Find the coordinates of a point above the line. Explain what the coordinates mean in this context.

    c. Find the coordinates of a point below the line. Explain what the coordinates mean in this context.

33. Frankie is looking forward to walking in a walkathon. She writes some equations to use to answer some questions she has. For each part below, tell what you think the equation might represent and write one question she could use it to answer.

    a. $y = 3x + 20$

    b. $y = 0.25x$

    c. $y = 4x$

Mathematical Reflections 1

In this investigation, you began to explore linear relationships by examining the patterns of change between two variables. The following questions will help you summarize what you have learned.

Think about your answers to these questions. Discuss your ideas with other students and your teacher. Then, write a summary of your findings in your notebook.

1. Describe how the dependent variable changes as the independent variable changes in a linear relationship. Give examples.

2. How does the pattern of change for a linear relationship show up in a table, a graph, and an equation of the relationship?

Investigation 2

Exploring Linear Functions With Graphs and Tables

In the last investigation, you examined relationships that were linear functions. For example, the *distance* a person walks at a constant rate is a function of the amount of *time* a person walks. The *amount of money* a person collects from a walkathon sponsor who pays a fixed amount per *kilometer* is a function of the distance walked. You used tables, graphs, and equations to answer questions about these relationships.

In this investigation, you will continue to solve problems involving linear functions.

2.1 Walking to Win

In Ms. Chang's class, Emile found out that his walking rate is 2.5 meters per second. When he gets home from school, he times his little brother Henri as Henri walks 100 meters. He figured out that Henri's walking rate is 1 meter per second.

Problem 2.1 Finding the Point of Intersection

Henri challenges Emile to a walking race. Because Emile's walking rate is faster, Emile gives Henri a 45-meter head start. Emile knows his brother would enjoy winning the race, but he does not want to make the race so short that it is obvious his brother will win.

A. How long should the race be so that Henri will win in a close race?

B. Describe your strategy for finding your answer to Question A. Give evidence to support your answer.

 ACE Homework starts on page 31.

2.2 Crossing the Line

Your class may have found some very interesting strategies for solving Problem 2.1, such as:

- Making a table showing time and distance data for both brothers
- Graphing time and distance data for both brothers on the same set of axes
- Writing an equation for each brother representing the relationship between time and distance

How can each of these strategies be used to solve the problem?

What other strategies were used in your class?

A. For each brother in Problem 2.1:

   1. Make a table showing the *distance from the starting line* at several different times during the first 40 seconds.

   2. Graph the time and the distance from the starting line on the same set of axes.

   3. Write an equation representing the relationship. Explain what information each variable and number represents.

B. 1. How far does Emile walk in 20 seconds?

   2. After 20 seconds, how far apart are the brothers? How is this distance represented in the table and on the graph?

   3. Is the point (26, 70) on either graph? Explain.

   4. When will Emile overtake Henri? Explain.

C. How can you determine which of two lines will be steeper

   1. from a table of the data?

   2. from an equation?

D. 1. At what points do Emile's and Henri's graphs cross the *y*-axis?

   2. What information do these points represent in terms of the race?

   3. How can these points be found in a table? In an equation?

 **Homework starts on page 31.**

Did You Know?

Have you ever seen a walking race? You may have thought the walking style of the racers seemed rather strange. Race walkers must follow two rules:

● The walker must always have one foot in contact with the ground.

● The walker's leg must be straight from the time it strikes the ground until it passes under the body.

A champion race walker can cover a mile in about 6.5 minutes. It takes most people 15 to 20 minutes to walk a mile.

Go Online
PHSchool.com **For:** Information about race-walking
Web Code: ane-9031

In the last problem, you found the point at which Emile's and Henri's graphs cross the *y*-axis. These points are called the *y-intercepts*.

- The distance d_{Emile} that Emile walks after *t* seconds can be represented by the equation, $d_{Emile} = 2.5t$. The *y*-intercept is $(0, 0)$ and the *coefficient* of *t* is 2.5.

- The distance d_{Henri} that Henri is from where Emile started can be given by the equation, $d_{Henri} = 45 + t$, where *t* is the time in seconds. The *y*-intercept is $(0, 45)$ and the *coefficient* of *t* is 1.

All of the linear equations we have studied so far can be written in the form $y = mx + b$ or $y = b + mx$. In this equation, *y* depends on *x*.

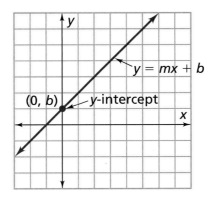

The **y-intercept** is the point where the line crosses the *y*-axis, or when $x = 0$. To save time, we sometimes refer to the number *b*, rather than the coordinates of the point $(0, b)$, as the *y*-intercept.

A **coefficient** is the number that multiplies a variable in an equation. The *m* in $y = mx + b$ is the coefficient of *x*, so *mx* means *m* times *x*.

Ms. Chang's class decides to give T-shirts to each person who participates in the Walkathon. They receive bids for the cost of the T-shirts from two different companies. Mighty Tee charges $49 plus $1 per T-shirt. No-Shrink Tee charges $4.50 per T-shirt. Ms. Chang writes the following equations to represent the relationship between cost and the number of T-shirts:

$$C_{Mighty} = 49 + n$$
$$C_{No\text{-}Shrink} = 4.5n$$

The number of T-shirts is n. C_{Mighty} is the cost in dollars for Mighty Tee and $C_{No\text{-}Shrink}$ is the cost in dollars for No-Shrink Tee.

A. 1. For each equation, explain what information the y-intercept and the coefficient of n represents.

    2. For each company, what is the cost for 20 T-shirts?

    3. Lani calculates that the school has about $120 to spend on T-shirts. From which company will $120 buy the most T-shirts?

    4. a. For what number of T-shirts is the cost of the two companies equal? What is that cost? Explain how you found the answers.

       b. How can this information be used to decide which plan to choose?

    5. Explain why the relationship between the cost and the number of T-shirts for each company is a linear relationship.

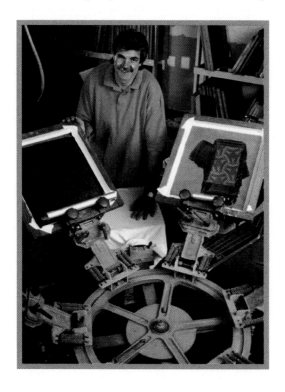

B. The table at the right represents the costs from another company, The Big T.

    1. Compare the costs for this company with the costs for the two companies in Question A.

    2. Does this plan represent a linear relationship? Explain.

    3. a. Could the point (20, 84) lie on the graph of this cost plan? Explain.

       b. What information about the number of T-shirts and cost do the coordinates of the point (20, 84) represent?

T-Shirt Costs

n	C
0	34
3	41.5
5	46.5
8	54
10	59

ACE   **Homework starts on page 31.**

2.4   Connecting Tables, Graphs, and Equations

Look again at Alana's pledge plan from Problem 1.3. Suppose A represents the dollars owed and d represents the number of kilometers walked. You can express this plan with the equation below:

$$\text{Alana's pledge plan: } A = 5 + 0.5d$$

Getting Ready for Problem **2.4**

- Explain why the point (14, 12) is on the graph of Alana's pledge plan.

- Write a question you could answer by locating this point.

- How can you use the equation for Alana's pledge plan to check the answer to the question you made up?

- How can you use a graph to find the number of kilometers that Alana walks if a sponsor pays her $17? How could you use an equation to answer this question?

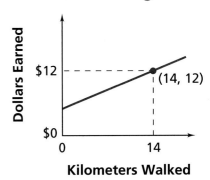

Alana's Pledge Plan

In the next problem, you will investigate similar questions relating to pledge plans for a walkathon.

Problem 2.4 Connecting Tables, Graphs, and Equations

Consider the following pledge plans. In each equation, y is the amount pledged in dollars, and x is the number of kilometers walked.

Plan 1 $y = 5x - 3$ Plan 2 $y = -x + 6$ Plan 3 $y = 2$

A. For each pledge plan:

1. What information does the equation give about the pledge plan? Does the plan make sense?

2. Make a table for values of x from -5 to 5.

3. Sketch a graph.

4. Do the y-values increase, decrease, or stay the same as the x-values increase?

B. Explain how you can use a graph, table, or equation to answer Question A, part (4).

C. 1. Which graph from Question A, part (3), can be traced to locate the point $(2, 4)$?

2. How do the coordinates $(2, 4)$ relate to the equation of the line? To the corresponding table of data?

3. Write a question you could answer by locating this point.

D. 1. Which equation has a graph you can trace to find the value of x that makes $8 = 5x - 3$ a true statement?

2. How does finding the value of x in $8 = 5x - 3$ help you find the coordinates for a point on the line of the equation?

E. The following three points all lie on the graph of the same plan:

   $(-7, 13)$ $(1.2, \blacksquare)$ $(\blacksquare, -4)$

1. Two of the points have a missing coordinate. Find the missing coordinate. Explain how you found it.

2. Write a question you could answer by finding the missing coordinate.

ACE Homework starts on page 31.

Applications

1. Grace and Allie are going to meet at the fountain near their houses. They both leave their houses at the same time. Allie passes Grace's house on her way to the fountain.

   - Allie's walking rate is 2 meters per second.
   - Grace's walking rate is 1.5 meters per second.

Allie's House   Grace's House   Fountain

|← —————————— 200 meters —————————— →|

   a. How many seconds will it take Allie to reach the fountain?

   b. Suppose Grace's house is 90 meters from the fountain. Who will reach the fountain first, Allie or Grace? Explain your reasoning.

2. In Problem 2.2, Emile's friend, Gilberto, joins the race. Gilberto has a head start of 20 meters and walks at 2 meters per second.

   a. Write an equation that gives the relationship between Gilberto's distance d from where Emile starts and the time, t.

   b. How would Gilberto's graph compare to Emile and Henri's graphs?

3. Ingrid stops at Tara's house on her way to school. Tara's mother says that Tara left 5 minutes ago. Ingrid leaves Tara's house, walking quickly to catch up with Tara. The graph below shows the distance each girl is from Tara's house, starting from the time Ingrid leaves Tara's house.

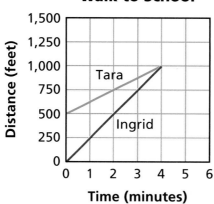

Tara's and Ingrid's Walk to School

a. In what way is this situation like the race between Henri and Emile? In what way is it different?

b. After how many minutes does Ingrid catch up with Tara?

c. How far from Tara's house does Ingrid catch up with Tara?

d. Each graph intersects the distance axis (the *y*-axis). What information do these points of intersection give about the problem?

e. Which line is steeper? How can you tell from the graph? How is the steepness of each line related to the rate at which the person travels?

f. What do you think the graphs would look like if we extended them to show distance and time after the girls meet?

4. A band decides to sell protein bars to raise money for an upcoming trip. The cost (the amount the band pays for the protein bars) and the income the band receives for the protein bars are represented on the graph below.

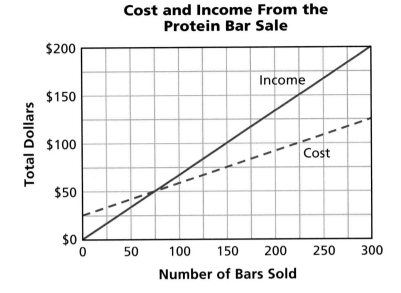

Cost and Income From the Protein Bar Sale

a. How many protein bars must be sold for the band's costs to equal the band's income?

b. What is the income from selling 50 protein bars? 125 bars?

c. Suppose the income is $200. How many protein bars were sold? How much of this income is profit?

Homework Help Online
PHSchool.com
For: Help with Exercise 4
Web Code: ane-5204

In Exercises 5 and 6, the student council asks for cost estimates for a skating party to celebrate the end of the school year.

5. The following tables represent the costs from two skating companies: Rollaway Skates and Wheelie's Skates and Stuff.

Rollaway Skates

Number of People	Cost
0	$0
1	$5
2	$10
3	$15
4	$20
5	$25
6	$30
7	$35
8	$40

Wheelie's Skates and Stuff

Number of People	Cost
0	$100
1	$103
2	$106
3	$109
4	$112
5	$115
6	$118
7	$121
8	$124

a. For each company, is the relationship between number of people and cost linear? Explain.

b. For each company, write an equation describing each cost plan.

c. Describe how you can use the table or graph to find when the costs of the two plans are equal. How can this information help the student council decide which company to choose?

6. A third company, Wheels to Go, gives their quote in the form of the equation $C_W = 35 + 4n$, where C_W is the cost in dollars for n students.

    a. What information do the numbers 35 and 4 represent in this situation?

    b. For 60 students, which of the three companies is the cheapest? Explain how you could determine the answer using tables, graphs, or equations.

    c. Suppose the student council wants to keep the cost of the skating party to $500. How many people can they invite under each of the three plans?

    d. The points below lie on one or more of the graphs of the three cost plans. Decide to which plan(s) each point belongs.

        i. $(20, 115)$ **ii.** $(65, 295)$ **iii.** $(50, 250)$

    e. Pick one of the points in part (d). Write a question that could be answered by locating this point.

7. Suppose each of the following patterns continues. Which are linear relationships? Explain your answer. For each pattern that is linear, write an equation that expresses the relationship.

a.

x	y
−10	−29
0	1
10	31
20	61
30	91

b.

x	y
1	9
5	17
7	21
20	47
21	49

c.

x	y
1	1
2	4
3	9
4	16
5	25

d.

x	y
1	9
5	22
7	25
20	56
21	60

8. The organizers of a walkathon get cost estimates from two printing companies to print brochures to advertise the event. The costs are given by the equations below, where C is the cost in dollars and n is the number of brochures.

$$\text{Company A: } C = 15 + 0.10n$$

$$\text{Company B: } C = 0.25n$$

a. For what number of brochures are the costs the same for both companies? What method did you use to get your answer?

b. The organizers have $65 to spend on brochures. How many brochures can they have printed if they use Company A? If they use Company B?

c. What information does the y-intercept represent for each equation?

d. What information does the coefficient of n represent for each equation?

9. A school committee is assigned the task of selecting a DJ for the end-of-school-year party. Susan obtains several quotes for the cost of three DJs.

Tom's Tunes charges $60 an hour.

Solidus' Sounds charges $100 plus $40 an hour.

Light Plastic charges $175 plus $30 an hour.

a. For each DJ, write an equation that shows how to calculate the total cost from the total number of hours.

b. What information does the coefficient of x represent for each DJ?

c. What information does the y-intercept represent for each DJ?

d. Suppose the DJ will need to work eight and one half hours. What is the cost of each DJ?

e. Suppose the committee has only $450 dollars to spend on a DJ. For how many hours could each DJ play?

10. A local department store offers two installment plans for buying a $270 skateboard.

    Plan 1: A fixed weekly payment of $10.80

    Plan 2: A $120 initial payment plus $6.00 per week

  a. For each plan, how much money is owed after 12 weeks?

  b. Which plan requires the least number of weeks to pay for the skateboard? Explain.

  c. Write an equation to represent each plan. Explain what information the variables and numbers represent.

  d. Suppose the skateboard costs $355. How would the answers to parts (a)–(c) change?

For each equation in Exercises 11–14, answer parts (a)–(d).

  a. What is the rate of change between the variables?

  b. State whether the y-values are increasing or decreasing, or neither, as x increases.

  c. Give the y-intercept.

  d. List the coordinates of two points that lie on a graph of the line of the equation.

Go Online
PHSchool.com
For: Multiple-Choice Skills Practice
Web Code: ana-5254

11. $y = 1.5x$

12. $y = -3x + 10$

13. $y = -2x + 6$

14. $y = 2x + 5$

15. Dani gets $7.50 per hour when she baby-sits.

  a. Draw a graph that represents the number of hours she baby-sits and the total amount of money she earns.

  b. Choose a point on the graph. Ask two questions that can be answered by finding the coordinates of this point.

16. Match each equation to a graph.

    a. $y = 3x + 5$ **b.** $y = x - 7$ **c.** $y = -x - 10$

Graph 1   **Graph 2**

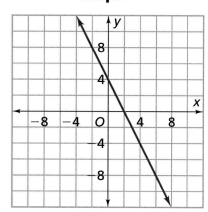 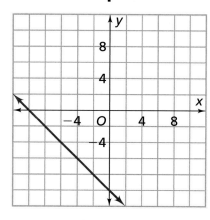

Graph 3   **Graph 4**

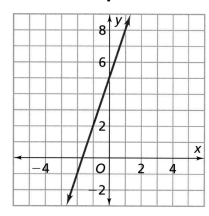 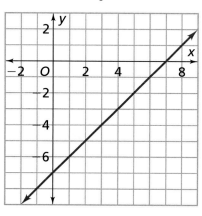

d. Write an equation for the graph that has no match.

17. Mary wants to use her calculator to find the value of x when $y = 22$ in the equation $y = 100 - 3x$. Explain how she can use each table or graph to find the value of x when $100 - 3x = 22$.

a.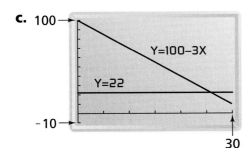

b.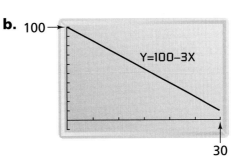

c.

100

Y=100–3X

Y=22

-10

30

For each equation in Exercises 18–21, give two values for x for which the value of y is negative.

18. $y = -2x - 5$

19. $y = -5$

20. $y = 2x - 5$

21. $y = \frac{3}{2}x - \frac{1}{4}$

For Exercises 22–28, consider the following equations:

   i. $y = 2x$ **ii.** $y = -5x$ **iii.** $y = 2x - 6$

   iv. $y = -2x + 1$ **v.** $y = 7$

22. Which equation has a graph you can trace to find the value of x that makes $8 = 2x - 6$ a true statement?

23. How does finding a solution to $8 = 2x - 6$ help you find the coordinates of a point on the line of the equation $y = 2x - 6$?

24. Which equation has a graph that contains the point $(7, -35)$?

25. The following two points lie on the graph that contains the point $(7, -35)$. Find the missing coordinate for each point.

     $(-1.2, \blacksquare)$ $(\blacksquare, -15)$

26. Which equations have a positive rate of change?

27. Which equations have a negative rate of change?

28. Which equations have a rate of change equal to zero?

Connections

29. The Ferry family decides to buy a new DVD player that costs $215. The store has an installment plan that allows them to make a $35 down payment and then pay $15 a month. The graph below shows the relationship between the number of months the family has had a DVD player and the amount they still owe.

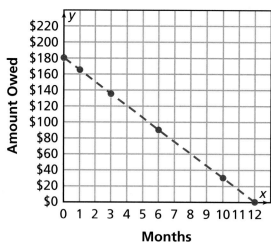

Paying for a DVD on an Installment Plan

a. Write an equation that represents the relationship between the amount the Ferry family still owes and the number of months after the purchase. Explain what information the numbers and variables represent.

b. The point where the graph of an equation intersects the x-axis is called the **x-intercept.** What are the x- and y-intercepts of the graph for this payment plan? Explain what information each intercept represents.

30. Use the Distributive Property to write two expressions that show two different ways to compute the area of each rectangle.

a.

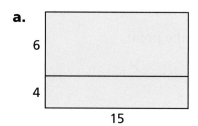

b.

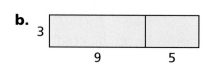

c.

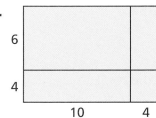

6

4

10   4

d.

x

4

8

31. Use the distributive property to write an expression equal to each of the following:

a. $x(-2 + 3)$ **b.** $(-4x) + (2x)$ **c.** $(x) - (4x)$

32. Decide whether each statement is true or false:

a. $15 - 3x = 15 + -3x$

b. $3.5x + 5 = 5(0.7x + 5)$

c. $3(2x + 1) = (2x + 1) + (2x + 1) + (2x + 1)$

33. Shallah Middle School is planning a school trip. The cost is $5 per person. The organizers know that three adults are going on the trip, but they do not yet know the number of students who will go. Write an expression that represents the total cost for x students and three adults.

34. Harvest Foods has apples on sale at 12 for $3.

a. What is the cost per apple?

b. Complete the rate table to show the costs of different numbers of apples.

The Cost of Apples

Number of Apples	12	▓	1	48	10	▓
Cost	$3	$1.50	▓	▓	▓	$4.50

c. How many apples can you buy for $1?

d. Is the relationship between number of apples and cost linear? Explain.

35. Ms. Peggy bought some bagels for her friends. She paid $15 for 20 bagels.

  a. How much did Ms. Peggy pay per bagel?

  b. Write an equation relating the number of bagels, n, to the total cost, c.

  c. Use your equation to find the cost of 150 bagels.

36. Ali says that $x = -1$ makes the equation $-8 = -3 + 5x$ true. Tamara checks this value for x in the equation. She says Ali is wrong because $-3 + 5 \times (-1)$ is -2, not -8. Why do you think these students disagree?

37. Determine whether the following mathematical sentences are true or false.

  a. $5 + 3 \times 2 = 16$ **b.** $3 \times 2 + 5 = 16$

  c. $5 + 3 \times 2 = 11$ **d.** $3 \times 2 + 5 = 11$

  e. $\frac{3}{2} \div \frac{4}{3} - \frac{1}{8} = 1$ **f.** $\frac{1}{2} + \frac{3}{2} \div \frac{1}{2} = 2$

38. Moesha feeds her dog the same amount of dog food each day from a very large bag. On the 3rd day, she has 44 cups left in the bag, and, on the 11th day, she has 28 cups left.

  a. How many cups of food does she feed her dog a day?

  b. How many cups of food were in the bag when she started?

  c. Write an equation for the total amount of dog food Moesha has left after feeding her dog for d days.

39. a. Match the following connecting paths for the last 5 minutes of Daren's race.

1.　　　2.　　　3.　　　4.　　　5.

   i.   Daren finishes running at a constant rate.

   ii. Daren runs slowly at first and gradually increases his speed.

  iii. Daren runs fast and then gradually decreases his speed.

   iv. Daren runs very fast and reaches the finish line early.

   v.   After falling, Daren runs at a constant rate.

  b. Which of the situations in part (a) was most likely to represent Daren's running for the race? Explain your answer.

40. In *Stretching and Shrinking*, you plotted the points $(8, 6)$, $(8, 22)$, and $(24, 14)$ on grid paper to form a triangle.

  a. Draw the triangle you get when you apply the rule $(0.5x, 0.5y)$ to the three points.

  b. Draw the triangle you get when you apply the rule $(0.25x, 0.25y)$ to the three points.

  c. How are the three triangles you have drawn related?

  d. What are the areas of the three triangles?

  e. Do you notice any linear relationships among the data of the three triangles, such as area, scale factor, lengths of sides, and so on?

41. In *Covering and Surrounding*, you looked at perimeters of rectangles.

  a. Make a table of possible whole number values for the length and width of a rectangle with a perimeter of 20 meters.

  b. What equation represents the data in this table? Make sure to define your variables.

  c. Is the relationship between length and width linear in this case?

  d. Find the area of each rectangle.

Extensions

42. Decide whether each equation represents a linear situation. Explain how you decided.

a. $y = 2x$ **b.** $y = \frac{2}{x}$ **c.** $y = x^2$

43. a. Write equations for three lines that intersect to form a triangle.

   b. Sketch the graphs and label the coordinates of the vertices of the triangle.

   c. Will any three lines intersect to form a triangle? Explain your reasoning.

44. a. Which one of the following points is on the line $y = 3x - 7$: $(3, 3)$, $(3, 2)$, $(3, 1)$, or $(3, 0)$? Describe where each of the other three points is in relation to the line.

   b. Find another point on the line $y = 3x - 7$ and three more points above the line.

   c. The points $(4, 5)$ and $(7, 14)$ lie on the graph of $y = 3x - 7$. Use this information to find two points that make the inequality $y < 3x - 7$ true and two points that make the inequality $y > 3x - 7$ true.

Mathematical Reflections 2

In this investigation, you continued to explore patterns of change in a linear relationship. You learned how to use tables and graphs to solve problems about linear relationships with equations of the form $y = mx + b$. The following questions will help you summarize what you have learned.

Think about your answers to these questions and discuss your ideas with other students and your teacher. Then write a summary of your findings in your notebook.

1. Summarize what you know about a linear relationship represented by an equation of the form $y = mx + b$.

2. **a.** Explain how a table or graph for a linear relationship can be used to solve a problem.

   b. Explain how you have used an equation to solve a problem.

Solving Equations

In the last investigation, you examined the patterns in the table and graph for the relationship between Alana's distance d and money earned A in the walkathon.

The equation $A = 5 + 0.5d$ is another way to represent the relationship between the distance and the money earned. The graph of this equation is a line that contains infinitely many points. The coordinates of the points on the line can be substituted into the equation to make a true statement.

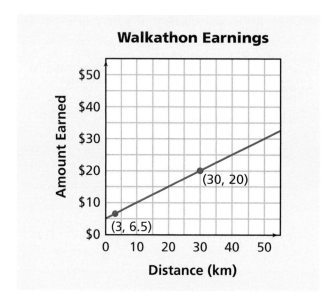

Walkathon Earnings

For example, the point $(3, 6.5)$ lies on the line. This means that $x = 3$ and $y = 6.5$. So, $6.5 = 5 + 0.5(3)$ is a true statement.

Similarly, the point $(30, 20)$ lies on the line which means that $x = 30$ and $y = 20$, and $20 = 5 + 0.5(30)$ is a true statement.

We say that $(3, 6.5)$ and $(30, 20)$ are *solutions* to the equation $A = 5 + 0.5d$ because when the values for d and A are substituted into the equation we get a true statement. There are infinitely many solutions to $A = 5 + 0.5d$.

Because the corresponding entries in a table are the coordinates of points on the line representing the equation, we can also find a solution to an equation by using a table.

d	A
0	5
1	5.5
2	6
3	6.5
4	7
20	15
25	17.5
30	20

3.1 Solving Equations Using Tables and Graphs

In an equation with two variables, if the value of one variable is known, you can use a table or graph to find the value of the other variable. For example, suppose Alana raises $10 from a sponsor. Then you can ask: How many kilometers does Alana walk?

In the equation $A = 5 + 0.5d$, this means that $A = 10$. The equation is now $10 = 5 + 0.5d$.

Which value of d *will make this a true statement?*

Finding the value of d that will make this a true statement is called *solving the equation* for d.

A. Use the equation $A = 5 + 0.5d$.

    1. Suppose Alana walks 23 kilometers. Show how you can use a table and a graph to find the amount of money Alana gets from each sponsor.

    2. Suppose Alana receives $60 from a sponsor. Show how you can use a table and a graph to find the number of kilometers she walks.

B. For each equation:

- Tell what information Alana is looking for.
- Describe how you can find the information.

    1. $A = 5 + 0.5(15)$

    2. $50 = 5 + 0.5d$

C. The following equations are related to situations that you have explored. Find the solution (the value of the variable) for each equation. Then, describe another way you can find the solution.

    1. $D = 25 + 2.5(7)$

    2. $70 = 25 + 2.5t$

ACE | **Homework starts on page 57.**

3.2 Exploring Equality

An equation states that two quantities are equal. In the equation $A = 5 + 0.5d$, A and $5 + 0.5d$ are the two quantities. Both represent the amount of money that Alana collects from each sponsor. Since each quantity represents numbers, you can use the properties of numbers to solve equations with one unknown variable.

Before we begin to solve linear equations, we need to look more closely at equality.

What does it mean for two quantities to be equal?

Let's look first at numerical statements.

The equation 85 = 70 + 15 states that the quantities 85 and 70 + 15 are equal.

What do you have to do to maintain equality if you

- subtract 15 from the left-hand side of the equation?
- add 10 to the right-hand side of the original equation?
- divide the left-hand side of the original equation by 5?
- multiply the right-hand side of the original equation by 4?

Try your methods on another example of equality. Summarize what you know about maintaining equality between two quantities.

In the Kingdom of Montarek, the ambassadors carry diplomatic pouches. The contents of the pouches are unknown except by the ambassadors. Ambassador Milton wants to send one-dollar gold coins to another country.

$1 gold coin   **diplomatic pouch**

His daughter, Sarah, is a mathematician. She helps him devise a plan based on *equality* to keep track of the number of one-dollar gold coins in each pouch.

In each situation:

- Each pouch contains the same number of one-dollar gold coins.
- The number of gold coins on both sides of the equality sign is the same, but some coins are hidden in the pouches.

Try to find the number of gold coins in each pouch.

A. Sarah draws the following picture. Each pouch contains the same number of $1 gold coins.

How many gold coins are in each pouch? Explain your reasoning.

B. For each situation, find the number of gold coins in the pouch. Write down your steps so that someone else could follow your steps to find the same number of coins in a pouch.

1.

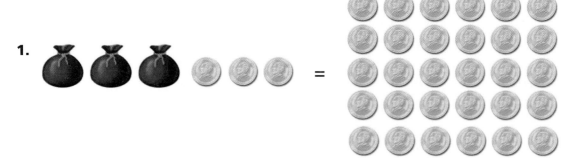

2.

3.

4.

5.

C. Describe how you can check your answer. That is, how do you know you found the correct number of gold coins in each pouch?

D. Describe how you maintained equality at each step of your solutions in Questions A and B.

ACE Homework starts on page 57.

3.3 From Pouches to Variables

Throughout this unit, you have been solving problems that involve two variables. Sometimes the value of one variable is known, and you want to find the value of the other variable. The next problem continues the search for finding a value for a variable without using a table or graph. In this investigation, you are learning to use *symbolic* methods to solve a linear equation.

Getting Ready for Problem **3.3**

The picture below represents another diplomatic pouch situation.

Because the number of gold coins in each pouch is unknown, we can let *x* represent the number of coins in one pouch and 1 represent the value of one gold coin.

- Write an equation to represent this situation.

- Use your methods from Problem 3.2 to find the number of gold coins in each pouch.

- Next to your work, write down a similar method using the equation that represents this situation.

A. For each situation:

- Represent the situation with an equation. Use an *x* to represent the number of gold coins in each pouch and a number to represent the number of coins on each side.

- Use the equation to find the number of gold coins in each pouch.

1.

2.

3.

4.

B. For each equation:

- Use your ideas from Question A to solve the equation.
- Check your answer.

1. $30 = 6 + 4x$

2. $7x = 5 + 5x$

3. $7x + 2 = 12 + 5x$

4. $2(x + 4) = 16$

C. Describe a general method for solving equations using what you know about equality.

ACE Homework starts on page 57.

3.4 Solving Linear Equations

You know that to maintain an equality, you can add, subtract, multiply, or divide both sides of the equality by the same number. These are called the **properties of equality.** In the last problem, you applied properties of equality and numbers to find a solution to an equation.

So far in this investigation, all of the situations have involved positive numbers.

Does it make sense to think about negative numbers in a coin situation?

Getting Ready for Problem 3.4

- How do these two equations compare?

$$2x + 10 = 16 \qquad 2x - 10 = 16$$

How would you solve each equation? That is, how would you find a value of x that makes each statement true?

- How do the equations below compare?

$$3x = 15 \qquad -3x = 15$$
$$3x = -15 \qquad -3x = -15$$

Find a value of x that makes each statement true.

Use what you have learned in this investigation to solve each equation.

For Questions A–D, record each step you take to find your solution and check your answer.

A. 1. $5x + 10 = 20$

    2. $5x - 10 = 20$

    3. $5x + 10 = -20$

    4. $5x - 10 = -20$

B. 1. $10 - 5x = 20$

    2. $10 - 5x = -20$

C. 1. $4x + 9 = 7x$

    2. $4x + 9 = 7x + 3$

    3. $4x - 9 = 7x$

    4. $4x - 9 = -7x + 13$

D. 1. $3(x + 2) = 21$

    2. $-3(x - 5) = 2x$

    3. $5(x + 2) = 6x + 3$

E. In all of the equations in Questions A–D, the value of x was an integer, but the solution to an equation can be any real number. Solve the equations below, and check your answers.

    1. $5x + 10 = 19$

    2. $5x + 10 = 9x$

    3. $5x - 10 = -19$

    4. $5x - 10 = -7x + 1$

F. 1. Describe how you could use a graph or table to solve the equation $5x + 10 = -20$.

    2. Suppose you use a different letter or symbol to represent the value of the unknown variable. For example, $5n + 10 = 6n$ instead of $5x + 10 = 6x$.

    Does this make a difference in solving the equation? Explain.

ACE Homework starts on page 57.

Finding the Point of Intersection

In Problem 2.3, you used the graphs (or tables) to find when the costs of two different plans for buying T-shirts were equal. The **point of intersection** of the two lines represented by the two graphs gives us information about when the costs of the two T-shirt plans are equal. The graphs of the two cost plans are shown below.

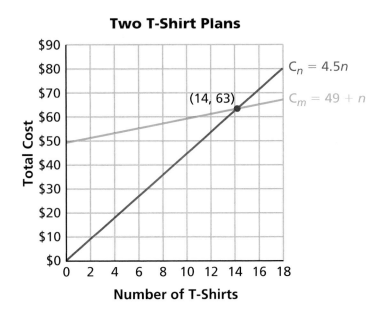

Two T-Shirt Plans

$C_n = 4.5n$

(14, 63)

$C_m = 49 + n$

C_m is the cost for Mighty Tee.

C_n is the cost for No-Shrink Tee.

Getting Ready for Problem 3.5

- What information do the coordinates of the point of intersection of the two graphs give you about this situation?

- For what number(s) of T-shirts is plan C_m less than plan C_n? ($C_m < C_n$)

- Show how you could use the two equations to find the coordinates of the point of intersection of the two lines ($C_m = C_n$).

At Fabulous Fabian's Bakery, the expenses E to make n cakes per month is given by the equation $E = 825 + 3.25n$.

The income I for selling n cakes is given by the equation $I = 8.20n$.

A. In the equations for I and E, what information do the y-intercepts represent? What about the coefficients of n?

B. Fabian sells 100 cakes in January.

   1. What are his expenses and his income?

   2. Does he make a profit? Describe how you found your answer.

C. In April, Fabian's expenses are $5,700.

   1. How many cakes does he sell?

   2. What is the income for producing this number of cakes?

   3. Does he make a profit? Explain.

D. The *break-even point* is when expenses equal income ($E = I$). Fabian thinks that this information is useful.

   1. Describe how you can find Fabian's break-even point symbolically. Find the break-even point.

   2. Describe another method for finding the break-even point.

ACE   **Homework starts on page 57.**

Applications

1. Ms. Chang's class decides to use the *Cool Tee's* company to make their T-shirts. The following equation represents the relationship between cost C and the number of T-shirts n.

$$C = 2n + 20$$

   a. The class wants to buy 25 T-shirts from *Cool Tee's*. Describe how you can use a table and a graph to find the cost for 25 T-shirts.

   b. Suppose the class has $80 to spend on T-shirts. Describe how you can use a table and a graph to find the number of T-shirts the class can buy.

   c. Sophia writes the following equation in her notebook:

   $$C = 2(15) + 20$$

   What information is Sophia looking for?

   d. Elisa uses the coordinates $(30, 80)$ to find information about the cost of the T-shirts. What information is she looking for?

2. The following equations represent some walkathon pledge plans.

   Plan 1: $14 = 2x$

   Plan 2: $y = 3.5(10) + 10$

   Plan 3: $100 = 1.5x + 55$

   In each equation, y is the amount owed in dollars, and x is the number of kilometers walked. For each equation:

   a. Tell what information is unknown.

   b. Describe how you could find the information.

3. Find the solution (the value of the variable for each equation).

   a. $y = 3(10) + 15$ b. $24 = x + 2$ c. $10 = 2x + 4$

4. Consider the equation: $y = 5x - 15$.

   a. Find y if $x = 1$.   b. Find x if $y = 50$.

   c. Describe how you can use a table or graph to answer parts (a) and (b).

Homework
Help **Online**
PHSchool.com

For: Help with Exercise 3
Web Code: ane-5303

For each situation in Exercises 5–8, find the number of coins in each pouch.

5.

6.

7.

8.

9. Rudo's grandfather gives Rudo $5 and then 50¢ for each math question he answers correctly on his math exams for the year.

    a. Write an equation that represents the amount of money that Rudo receives during a school year. Explain what the variables and numbers mean.

    b. Use the equation to find the number of correct answers Rudo needs to buy a new shirt that costs $25. Show your work.

    c. Rudo answered all 12 problems correctly on his first exam. How much money is he assured of receiving for the year? Show your work.

10. For each equation, sketch a picture using pouches and coins, and then determine how many coins are in a pouch.

    a. $3x = 12$ **b.** $2x + 5 = 19$

    c. $4x + 5 = 2x + 19$ **d.** $x + 12 = 2x + 6$

    e. $3(x + 4) = 18$

11. For parts (a) and (b), find the mystery number and explain your reasoning.

   a. If you add 15 to 3 times the mystery number, you get 78. What is the mystery number?

   b. If you subtract 27 from 5 times the mystery number, you get 83. What is the mystery number?

   c. Make up clues for a riddle whose mystery number is 9.

12. Use properties of equality and numbers to solve each equation for x. Check your answers.

   a. $7 + 3x = 5x + 13$ **b.** $3x - 7 = 5x + 13$

   c. $7 - 3x = 5x + 13$ **d.** $3x + 7 = 5x - 13$

13. Multiple Choice Which of the following is a solution to the equation $11 = -3x - 10$?

   A. 1.3   **B.** $-\frac{1}{3}$ **C.** -7 **D.** 24

14. Use properties of equality and numbers to solve each equation for x. Check your answers.

For: Multiple-Choice Skills Practice
Web Code: ana-5354

   a. $3x + 5 = 20$ **b.** $3x - 5 = 20$

   c. $3x + 5 = -20$ **d.** $-3x + 5 = 20$

   e. $-3x - 5 = -20$

15. Solve each equation. Check your answers.

   a. $3(x + 2) = 12$ **b.** $3(x + 2) = x - 18$

   c. $3(x + 2) = 2x$ **d.** $3(x + 2) = -15$

16. Two students' solutions to the equation $6(x + 4) = 3x - 2$ are shown. Both students made an error. Find the errors and give a correct solution.

Student 1	Student 2
$6(x + 4) = 3x - 2$	$6(x + 4) = 3x - 2$
$x + 4 = 3x - 2 - 6$	$6x + 4 = 3x - 2$
$x + 4 = 3x - 8$	$3x + 4 = -2$
$x + 4 + 8 = 3x - 8 + 8$	$3x + 4 - 4 = -2 - 4$
$x + 12 = 3x$	$3x = -6$
$12 = 2x$	$x = -2$ ✗
$x = 6$ ✗	

17. Two students' solutions to the equation $58.5 = 3.5x - 6$ are shown below. Both students made an error. Find the errors and give a correct solution.

Student 1

$58.5 = 3.5x - 6$

$58.5 - 6 = 3.5x$

$52.5 = 3.5x$

$\dfrac{52.5}{3.5} = x$

so, $x = 15$ ✗

Student 2

$58.5 = 3.5x - 6$

$58.5 + 6 = 3.5x - 6 + 6$

$64.5 = 3.5x$

$\dfrac{64.5}{3.5} = \dfrac{3.5}{3.5} x$

so, $x \approx 1.84$ ✗

For Exercises 18 and 19, use the equation $y = 4 - 3x$.

18. Find y if

  a. $x = 4$ **b.** $x = -3$ **c.** $x = 2$

  d. $x = -\dfrac{4}{3}$ **e.** $x = 0$

19. Find x when:

  a. $y = 0$ **b.** $y = 21$

  c. $y = -15$ **d.** $y = 3.5$

20. Explain how the information you found for Exercises 18 and 19 relates to locating points on a line representing $y = 4 - 3x$.

21. Use the equation $P = 10 - 2.5c$.

  a. Find P when $c = 3.2$.   **b.** Find c when $P = 85$.

  c. Describe how you can use a table or graph to answer parts (a) and (b).

22. Use the equation $m = 15.75 + 3.2d$.

  a. Find m when:

   i. $d = 20$ **ii.** $d = 0$ **iii.** $d = 3.2$

  b. Find d when:

   i. $m = 54.15$ **ii.** $m = 0$ **iii.** $m = 100$

23. Forensic scientists can estimate a person's height by measuring the length of certain bones, including the femur, the tibia, the humerus, and the radius.

The table below gives equations for the relationships between the length of each bone and the estimated height of males and females. These relationships were found by scientists after much study and data collection.

In the table, F represents the length of the femur, T the length of the tibia, H the length of the humerus, R the length of the radius, and h the person's height. All measurements are in centimeters.

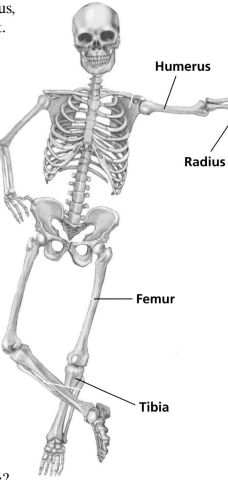

Humerus

Radius

Bone	Male	Female
Femur	$h = 69.089 + 2.238F$	$h = 61.412 + 2.317F$
Tibia	$h = 81.688 + 2.392T$	$h = 72.572 + 2.533T$
Humerus	$h = 73.570 + 2.970H$	$h = 64.977 + 3.144H$
Radius	$h = 80.405 + 3.650R$	$h = 73.502 + 3.876R$

a. About how tall is a female if her femur is 46.2 centimeters long?

b. About how tall is a male if his tibia is 50.1 centimeters long?

c. Suppose a woman is 152 centimeters tall. About how long is her femur? Her tibia? Her humerus? Her radius?

d. Suppose a man is 183 centimeters tall. About how long is his femur? His tibia? His humerus? His radius?

e. Describe what the graphs would look like for each equation. What do the x- and y-intercepts represent in this problem? Does this make sense? Why?

Femur

Tibia

24. The costs C and income I for making and selling T-shirts with a school logo are given by the equations $C = \$535 + 4.50n$ and $I = \$12n$, where n is the number of T-shirts.

a. How many T-shirts must be bought and sold to break even? Explain.

b. Suppose only 50 shirts are sold. Is there a profit or loss? Explain.

c. Suppose the income is $1,200. Is there a profit or loss? Explain.

d. i. For each equation, find the coordinates of a point that lies on the graph of the equation.

ii. What information does this point give?

iii. Describe how to use the equation to see that the point will be on the graph.

25. The International Links long-distance phone company charges no monthly fee but charges 18 cents per minute for long-distance calls. The World Connections long distance company charges $50 per month plus 10 cents per minute for long-distance calls. Compare the World Connections long-distance plan to that of International Links. Under what circumstances is it cheaper to use International Links? Explain your reasoning.

26. Students at Hammond Middle School are raising money for the end-of-year school party. They decide to sell roses for Valentine's Day. The students can buy the roses for 50 cents each from a wholesaler. They also need $60 to buy ribbon and paper to protect the roses as well as materials for advertising the sale. They sell each rose for $1.30.

a. How many roses must they sell to break even? Explain.

b. How much profit is there if they sell 50 roses? 100 roses? 200 roses?

27. Ruth considers two different cable television plans. Company A has a cost plan represented by the equation $C_A = 32N$, where N is the number of months she has the plan and C_A is the total cost. Company B has a cost plan represented by the equation $C_B = 36 + 26N$, where N is the number of months she is on the plan and C_B is the total cost.

   a. Graph both equations on the same axis.

   b. What is the point of intersection of the two graphs? What information does this give us?

Connections

28. Describe what operations are indicated in each expression, then write each expression as a single number.

   a. $-8(4)$ **b.** $-2 \cdot 4$

   c. $6(-5) - 10$ **d.** $2(-2) + 3(5)$

29. Decide whether each pair of quantities is equal. Explain.

   a. $6(5) + 2$ and $6(5 + 2)$ **b.** $8 - 3x$ and $3x - 8$

   c. $4 + 5$ and $5 + 4$ **d.** $-2(3)$ and $3(-2)$

   e. $3 - 5$ and $5 - 3$ **f.** 2 quarters and 5 dimes

   g. 1.5 liters and 15 milliliters

   h. 2 out of 5 students prefer wearing sneakers to school and 50% of the students prefer wearing sneakers to school

30. a. Use your knowledge about fact families to write a related sentence for $n - (-3) = 30$. Does this related sentence make it easier to find the value for n? Why or why not?

   b. Write a related sentence for $5 + n = -36$. Does this related sentence make it easier to find the value for n? Why or why not?

31. Write two different expressions to represent the area of each rectangle.

   a. 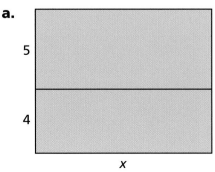   **b.**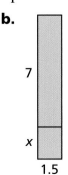

32. Find each quotient.

a. $\dfrac{12}{-3}$ b. $\dfrac{-12}{3}$ c. $\dfrac{-12}{-3}$ d. $\dfrac{0}{-10}$

e. $\dfrac{-5}{5}$ f. $\dfrac{5}{-5}$ g. $\dfrac{-5}{-5}$

33. Find the value of x that makes each equation true.

a. $3\dfrac{1}{2}x = \dfrac{3}{4}$ b. $3\dfrac{1}{2} = \dfrac{3}{4}x$

c. $\dfrac{7}{8}x = \dfrac{1}{8}$ d. $\dfrac{5}{6} = \dfrac{3}{4}x$

34. The sum S of the angles of a polygon with n sides is $S = 180(n - 2)$. Find the angle sum of each polygon.

     a. triangle   b. quadrilateral   c. hexagon

     d. decagon (10-sided polygon)

     e. icosagon (20-sided polygon)

35. Suppose the polygons in Exercise 34 are regular polygons. Find the measure of an interior angle of each polygon.

36. How many sides does a polygon have if its angle sum is

     a. 540 degrees   b. 1,080 degrees

37. The perimeter of each shape is 24 cm. Find the value of x.

a.
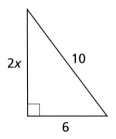
2, 5x

b.
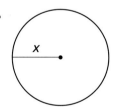
x

c.

2x, 10, 6

     d. Find the area of each figure in parts (a)–(c).

38. World Connections long-distance phone company charges $50 per month plus 10¢ per minute for each call.

   a. Write an equation for the total monthly cost C for t minutes of long-distance calls.

   b. A customer makes $10\frac{1}{2}$ hours of long-distance calls in a month. How much is his bill for that month?

   c. A customer receives a $75 long-distance bill for last month's calls. How many minutes of long-distance calls did she make?

39. The number of times a cricket chirps in a minute is a function of the temperature. You can use the formula

$$n = 4t - 160$$

to determine the number of chirps n a cricket makes in a minute when the temperature is t degrees Fahrenheit. If you want to estimate the temperature by counting cricket chirps, you can use the following form of the equation:

$$t = \frac{1}{4}n + 40$$

   a. At 60°F, how many times does a cricket chirp in a minute?

   b. What is the temperature if a cricket chirps 150 times in a minute?

   c. At what temperature does a cricket stop chirping?

   d. Sketch a graph of the equation with number of chirps on the x-axis and temperature on the y-axis. What information do the y-intercept and the coefficient of n give you?

40. The higher the altitude, the colder the temperature. The formula $T = t - \frac{d}{150}$ is used to estimate the temperature T at different altitudes, where t is the ground temperature in degrees Celsius (Centigrade) and d is the altitude in meters.

    a. Suppose the ground temperature is 0 degrees Celsius. What is the temperature at an altitude of 1,500 meters?

    b. Suppose the temperature at 300 meters is 26 degrees Celsius. What is the ground temperature?

41. As a person ages beyond 30, his or her height can start to decrease by approximately 0.06 centimeter per year.

    a. Write an equation that represents a person's height h after the age of 30. Let t be the number of years beyond 30 and H be the height at age 30.

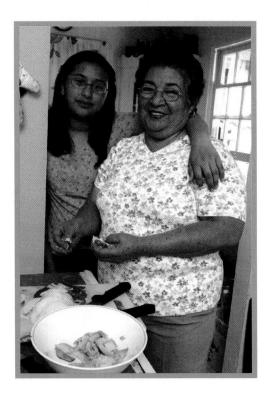

    b. Suppose a 60- to 70-year-old grandmother is 160 centimeters tall. About how tall was she at age 30? Explain how you found your answer.

    c. Suppose a basketball player is 6 feet, 6 inches tall on his thirtieth birthday. About how tall will he be at age 80? (Remember, 1 inch $\approx$ 2.54 centimeters.) Explain.

Extensions

42. The Small World long-distance phone company charges 55¢ for the first minute of a long-distance call and 23¢ for each additional minute.

   a. Write an equation for the total cost C of an m-minute long-distance call. Explain what your variables and numbers mean.

   b. How much does a 10-minute long-distance call cost?

   c. Suppose a call costs $4.55. How long does the call last?

43. The maximum weight allowed in an elevator is 1,500 pounds.

   a. The average weight per adult is 150 pounds, and the average weight per child is 40 pounds. Write an equation for the number of adults A and the number of children C the elevator can hold.

   b. Suppose ten children are in the elevator. How many adults can get in?

   c. Suppose six adults are in the elevator. How many children can get in?

44. Solve each equation for x. Check your answers.

   a. $5 - 2(x - 1) = 12$

   b. $5 + 2(x - 1) = 12$

   c. $5 - 2(x + 2) = 12$

   d. $5 - 2x + 2 = 12$

45. Solve each equation for x. Explain what your answers might mean.

   a. $2(x + 3) = 3x + 3$ **b.** $2(x + 3) = 2x + 6$

   c. $2(x + 3) = 2x + 3$

46. Wind can affect the speed of an airplane. Suppose a plane is flying round-trip from New York City to San Francisco. The plane has a cruising speed of 300 miles per hour. The wind is blowing from west to east at 30 miles per hour.

When the plane flies into (in the opposite direction of) the wind, its speed decreases by 30 miles per hour. When the plane flies with (in the same direction as) the wind, its speed increases by 30 miles per hour.

a. The distance between New York City and San Francisco is 3,000 miles. Make a table that shows the total time the plane has traveled after each 200-mile interval on its trip from New York City to San Francisco and back.

Airplane Flight Times

Distance (mi)	NYC to SF Time (h)	SF to NYC Time (h)
0	■	■
200	■	■
400	■	■
600	■	■
■	■	■

b. For each direction, write an equation for the distance d traveled in t hours.

c. On the same set of axes, sketch graphs of the time and distance data for travel in both directions.

d. How long does it take a plane to fly 5,000 miles against a 30-mile-per-hour wind? With a 30-mile-per-hour wind? Explain how you found your answers.

Mathematical Reflections 3

In this investigation, you learned how to solve equations by operating on the symbols. These questions will help you summarize what you have learned.

Think about your answers to these questions. Discuss your ideas with other students and your teacher. Then, write a summary of your findings in your notebook.

1. Describe a symbolic method for solving a linear equation. Use an example to illustrate the method.

2. Compare the symbolic method for solving linear equations to the methods of using a table or graph.

Investigation 4

Exploring Slope

All of the patterns of change you have explored in this unit involved constant rates. For example, you worked with walking rates expressed as meters per second and pledge rates expressed as dollars per mile. In these situations, you found that the rate affects the following things:

- the steepness of the graph
- the coefficient, *m*, of *x* in the equation $y = mx + b$
- how the *y*-values in the table change for each unit change in the *x*-values

In this investigation, you will explore another way to express the constant rate.

4.1 Climbing Stairs

Climbing stairs is good exercise, so some athletes run up and down stairs as part of their training. The steepness of stairs determines how difficult they are to climb. By investigating the steepness of stairs you can find another important way to describe the steepness of a line.

Getting Ready for Problem 4.1

Consider these questions about the stairs you use at home, in your school, and in other buildings.

- How can you describe the steepness of the stairs?
- Is the steepness the same between any two consecutive steps?

Carpenters have developed the guidelines below to ensure that the stairs they build are relatively easy for a person to climb. Steps are measured in inches.

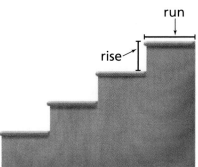

- The ratio of rise to run for each step should be between 0.45 and 0.60.

- The rise plus the run for each step should be between 17 and $17\frac{1}{2}$ inches.

The steepness of stairs is determined by the ratio of the rise to the run for each step. The rise and run are labeled in the diagram at the right.

Problem 4.1 Using Rise and Run

A. 1. Determine the steepness of a set of stairs in your school or home. To calculate the steepness you will need to

- measure the rise and run of at least two steps in the set of stairs.
- make a sketch of the stairs, and label the sketch with the measurements you found.
- find the ratio of rise to run.

2. How do the stairs you measured compare to the carpenters' guidelines above?

B. A set of stairs is being built for the front of the new Arch Middle School. The ratio of rise to run is 3 to 5.

1. Is this ratio within the carpenters' guidelines?

2. Make a sketch of a set of stairs that meet this ratio. Label the lengths of the rise and run of a step.

3. Sketch the graph of a line that passes through the origin and whose y-values change by 3 units for each 5-unit change in the x-values.

4. Write an equation for the line in part (3).
   a. What is the coefficient of x in the equation?
   b. How is the coefficient related to the steepness of the line represented by the equation?
   c. How is the coefficient related to the steepness of a set of stairs with this ratio?

ACE Homework starts on page 78.

4.2 Finding the Slope of a Line

The method for finding the steepness of stairs suggests a way to find the steepness of a line. A line drawn from the bottom step of a set of stairs to the top step touches each step in one point. The rise and the run of a step are the vertical and the horizontal changes, respectively, between two points on the line.

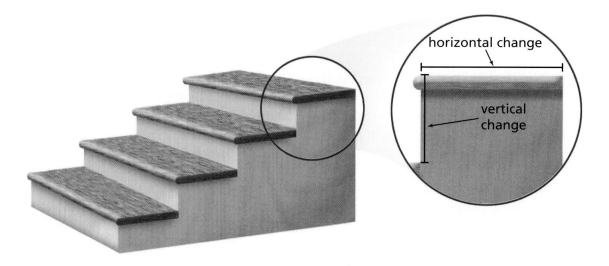

The steepness of the line is the ratio of rise to run, or vertical change to horizontal change, for this step. We call this ratio the **slope** of the line.

$$\text{slope} = \frac{\text{vertical change}}{\text{horizontal change}} \quad \text{or} \quad \frac{\text{rise}}{\text{run}}$$

Unlike the steepness of stairs, the slope of a line can be negative. To determine the slope of a line, you need to consider the direction, or sign, of the vertical and horizontal changes from one point to another. If vertical change is negative for positive horizontal change, the slope will be negative. Lines that slant *upward* from left to right have *positive slope*; lines that slant *downward* from left to right have *negative slope*.

• For each graph, describe how you can find the slope of the line.

**Line With
Positive Slope**

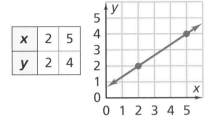

x	2	5
y	2	4

**Line With
Negative Slope**

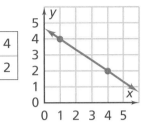

x	1	4
y	4	2

• The data in the table represent a linear relationship. Describe how you can find the slope of the line that represents the data.

x	−1	0	1	2	3	4
y	0	3	6	9	12	15

Information about a linear situation can be given in several different representations, such as a table, graph, equation, or verbal situation. These representations are useful in answering questions about linear situations.

How can we calculate the slope of a line from these representations?

A. The graphs, tables and equations all represent linear situations.

Graph 1 **Graph 2**

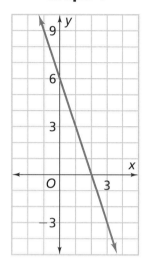 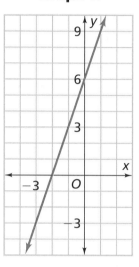

Table 1

x	−6	−4	−2	0	2	4
y	−10	−7	−4	−1	2	5

Table 2

x	1	2	3	4	5	6
y	4.5	4.0	3.5	3.0	2.5	2.0

Equation 1 **Equation 2**
$y = 2.5x + 5$ $y = 20 - 3x$

1. Find the slope and y-intercept of the line represented in each situation.

2. Write an equation for each graph and table.

B. The points $(3, 5)$ and $(-2, 10)$ lie on a line. Find two more points that lie on this line. Explain your method.

C. Compare your methods for finding the slope of a line from a graph, table, and equation.

ACE Homework starts on page 78.

4.3 Exploring Patterns With Lines

Your understanding of linear relationships can be used to explore some ideas about groups of lines.

Getting Ready for **Problem** 4.3

The slope of a line is 3.

- Sketch a line with this slope.
- Can you sketch a different line with this slope? Explain.

Problem 4.3 Exploring Patterns With Lines

A. Consider the two groups of lines shown below.

Group 1: $y = 3x$ $y = 5 + 3x$ $y = 10 + 3x$ $y = -5 + 3x$
Group 2: $y = -2x$ $y = 4 - 2x$ $y = 8 - 2x$ $y = -4 - 2x$

For each group:

1. What features do the equations have in common?

2. Graph each equation on the same coordinate axes. What patterns do you observe in the graphs?

3. Describe another group of lines that have the same pattern.

B. Consider the three pairs of lines shown below.

Pair 1: $y = 2x$ Pair 2: $y = 4x$ Pair 3: $y = -3x + 5$
         $y = -\frac{1}{2}x$ $y = -0.25x$ $y = \frac{1}{3}x - 1$

For each pair:

1. What features do the equations have in common?

2. Graph each equation on the same coordinate axes. What patterns do you observe in the graphs?

3. Describe another pair of lines that have the same pattern.

C. Write equations for four lines that intersect to form the sides of a parallelogram. Explain what must be true about such lines.

D. Write equations for three lines that intersect to form a right triangle. Explain what must be true about such lines.

E. Describe how you can decide if two lines are parallel or perpendicular from the equations of the lines.

ACE **Homework starts on page 78.**

Throughout this unit, you have learned several ways to represent linear relationships. You have also learned ways to move back and forth between these representations, tables, graphs, and equations to solve problems. The next problem pulls some of these ideas together.

Problem 4.4 Writing Equations With Two Variables

A. Anjelita's Birthday

Today is Anjelita's birthday. Her grandfather gave Anjelita some money as a birthday gift. Anjelita plans to put her birthday money in a safe place and add part of her allowance to it each week. Her sister, Maria, wants to know how much their grandfather gave her and how much of her allowance she is planning to save each week. As usual, Anjelita does not answer her sister directly. Instead, she wants her to figure out the answer for herself. She gives her these clues:

- After five weeks, I will have saved a total of $175.
- After eight weeks, I will have saved $190.

1. How much of her allowance is Anjelita planning to save each week?

2. How much birthday money did Anjelita's grandfather give her for her birthday?

3. Write an equation for the total amount of money A Anjelita will have saved after n weeks. What information do the y-intercept and coefficient of n represent in this context?

B. Converting Temperatures

Detroit, Michigan, is just across the Detroit River from the Canadian city of Windsor, Ontario. Because Canada uses the Celsius temperature scale, weather reports in Detroit often give temperatures in both degrees Fahrenheit and in degrees Celsius. The relationship between degrees Fahrenheit and degrees Celsius is linear.

Two important reference points for temperature are:

- Water freezes at 0°C, or 32°F.
- Water boils at 100°C, or 212°F.

   1. Use this information to write an equation for the relationship between degrees Fahrenheit and degrees Celsius.

   2. How did you find the *y*-intercept? What does the *y*-intercept tell you about this situation?

Mon	Tues	Wed	Thurs	Fri
55° F	58° F	63° F	70° F	58° F
13° C	14° C	17° C	21° C	14° C

ACE Homework starts on page 78.

Applications

1. Plans for a set of stairs for the front of a new community center use the ratio of rise to run of 2 units to 5 units.

   a. Are these stairs within carpenters' guidelines, which state that the ratio of rise to run should be between 0.45 and 0.60?

   b. Sketch a set of stairs that meets the rise-to-run ratio of 2 units to 5 units.

   c. Sketch the graph of a line where the y-values change by 2 units for each 5-unit change in the x-values.

   d. Write an equation for your line in part (c).

2. a. Find the horizontal distance and the vertical distance between the two points at the right.

   b. What is the slope of the line?

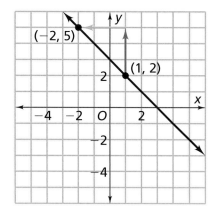

3. Seven possible descriptions of lines are listed below.

   i. positive slope   **ii.** negative slope

   iii. y-intercept equals 0   **iv.** passes through the point $(1, 2)$

   v. slope of zero   **vi.** positive y-intercept

   vii. negative y-intercept

For each equation, list *all* of the descriptions i–vii that describe the graph of that equation.

   a. $y = 2x$ **b.** $y = 3 - 3x$

   c. $y = 2x + 3$ **d.** $y = 5x - 3$

   e. $y = 2$

For Exercises 4–7, find the slope and the y-intercept of the line associated with the equation.

   4. $y = 10 + 3x$ **5.** $y = 0.5x$

   6. $y = -3x$ **7.** $y = -5x + 2$

In Exercises 8–12, the tables represent linear relationships. Give the slope and the y-intercept of the graph of each relationship. Then determine which of the five equations listed below fits each relationship.

$y = 5 - 2x$ $y = 2x$ $y = -3x - 5$

$y = 2x - 1$ $y = x + 3.5$

Homework Help Online
PHSchool.com
For: Help with
    Exercises 8–12
Web Code: ane-5408

8.

x	0	1	2	3	4
y	0	2	4	6	8

9.

x	0	1	2	3	4
y	3.5	4.5	5.5	6.5	7.5

10.

x	1	2	3	4	5
y	1	3	5	7	9

11.

x	0	1	2	3	4
y	5	3	1	-1	-3

12.

x	2	3	4	5	6
y	-11	-14	-17	-20	-23

13. a. Find the slope of the line represented by the equation
$y = x - 1$.

   b. Make a table of x- and y-values for the equation $y = x - 1$.
   How is the slope related to the table entries?

14. a. Find the slope of the line represented by the equation
$y = -2x + 3$.

   b. Make a table of x- and y-values for the equation $y = -2x + 3$.
   How is the slope related to the table entries?

15. In parts (a) and (b), the equations represent linear relationships.
Use the given information to find the value of b.

   a. The point $(1, 5)$ lies on the line representing $y = b - 3.5x$.

   b. The point $(0, -2)$ lies on the line representing $y = 5x - b$.

   c. What are the y-intercepts in the linear relationships in parts (a) and
   (b)? What are the patterns of change for the linear relationships in
   parts (a) and (b)?

   d. Find the x-intercepts for the linear relationships in parts (a) and (b).
   (The x-intercept is the point where the graph intersects the x-axis.)

For each pair of points in Exercises 16–19, do parts (a)–(e).

   a. Plot the points on a coordinate grid and draw a line through them.

   b. Find the slope of the line.

   c. Find the y-intercept from the graph. Explain how you found the
   y-intercept.

   d. Use your answers from parts (b) and (c) to write an equation for
   the line.

   e. Find one more point that lies on the line.

16. $(0, 0)$ and $(3, 3)$ **17.** $(-1, 1)$ and $(3, -3)$

18. $(0, -5)$ and $(-2, -3)$ **19.** $(3, 6)$ and $(5, 6)$

For Exercises 20–22, determine which of the linear relationships A–K fit each description.

A.

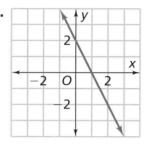

B.

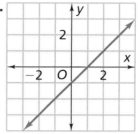

C.

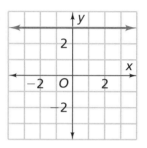

D.

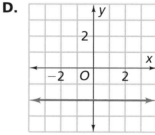

E.

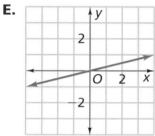

F.

x	−3	−2	−1	0
y	7	5	3	1

G.

x	−4	−2	−1	0
y	2	2	2	2

H. $y = 1.5$ **J.** $y = -5 + 3x$ **K.** $y = 4 + -2x$

20. The line representing this relationship has positive slope.

21. The line representing this relationship has a slope of −2.

22. The line representing this relationship has a slope of 0.

Go Online
PHSchool.com
For: Multiple-Choice Skills Practice
Web Code: ana-5454

23. Decide which graph from Exercises 20–22 matches each equation.

     a. $y = x - 1$ **b.** $y = -2$ **c.** $y = \frac{1}{4}x$

For each equation in Exercises 24–26, do parts (a)–(d).

24. $y = x$ **25.** $y = 2x - 2$ **26.** $y = -0.5x + 2$

     a. Make a table of x- and y-values for the equation.

     b. Sketch a graph of the equation.

     c. Find the slope of the line.

     d. Make up a problem that can be represented by each equation.

27. a. Graph a line with slope 3.

       i. Find two points on your line.

       ii. Write an equation for the line.

     b. On the same set of axes, graph a line with slope $-\frac{1}{3}$.

       i. Find two points on your line.

       ii. Write an equation for the line.

     c. Compare the two graphs you made in parts (a) and (b).

28. Use the line in the graph below to answer each question.

     a. Find the equation for a line that is parallel to this line.

     b. Find the equation of a line that is perpendicular to this line.

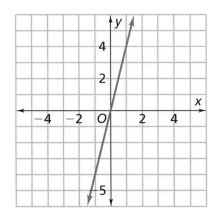

29. Descriptions of three possible lines are listed below.

     • a line that *does not* pass through the first quadrant

     • a line that passes through exactly two quadrants

     • a line that passes through only one quadrant

     a. For each, decide whether such a line exists. Explain.

     b. If a line exists, what must be true about the equation of the line that satisfies the conditions?

     c. Sketch a graph, then write the equation of the line next to the graph.

30. a. Find the slope of each line. Then, write an equation for the line.

i.

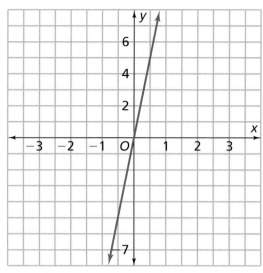

ii.

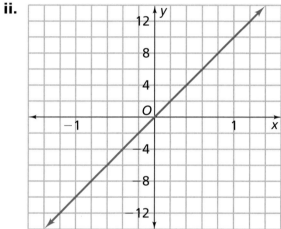

iii.

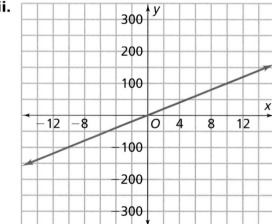

b. Compare the slopes of the three lines.

c. How are the three graphs similar? How are they different?

31. The slopes of two lines are the negative reciprocal of each other. For example:

$$y = 2x \qquad \text{and} \qquad y = -\frac{1}{2}x$$

What must be true about the two lines? Is your conjecture true if the y-intercept of either equation is not zero? Explain.

32. At noon, the temperature is 30°F. For the next several hours, the temperature falls by an average of 3°F an hour.

a. Write an equation for the temperature T, n hours after noon.

b. What is the y-intercept of the line the equation represents? What does the y-intercept tell us about this situation?

c. What is the slope of the line the equation represents? What does the slope tell us about this situation?

33. Natasha never manages to make her allowance last for a whole week, so she borrows money from her sister. Suppose Natasha borrows 50 cents every week.

a. Write an equation for the amount of money m Natasha owes her sister after n weeks.

b. What is the slope of the graph of the equation from part (a)?

34. In 1990, the small town of Cactusville was destined for obscurity. However, due to hard work by its city officials, it began adding manufacturing jobs at a fast rate. As a result, the city's population grew 239% from 1990 to 2000. The population of Cactusville in 2000 was 37,000.

a. What was the population of Cactusville in 1990?

b. Suppose the same rate of population increase continues. What might the population be in the year 2010?

35. James and Shani share a veterinary practice. They each make farm visits two days a week. They take cellular phones on these trips to keep in touch with the office. James makes his farm visits on weekdays. His cellular phone rate is $14.95 a month plus $0.50 a minute. Shani makes her visits on Saturday and Sunday and is charged a weekend rate of $34 a month.

a. Write an equation for each billing plan.

b. Is it possible for James's cellular phone bill to be more than Shani's? Explain how you know this.

c. Suppose James and Shani made the same number of calls in the month of May. Is it possible for James's and Shani's phone bills to be for the same amount? If so, how many minutes of phone calls would each person have to make for their bills to be equal?

d. Shani finds another phone company that offers one rate for both weekday and weekend calls. The billing plan for this company can be expressed by the equation $A = 25 + 0.25m$, where A is the total monthly bill and m is the number of minutes of calls. Compare this billing plan with the other two plans.

Connections

36. In Europe, many hills have signs indicating their steepness, or slope. Two examples are shown at the right.

On a coordinate grid, sketch hills with each of these slopes.

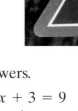

37. Solve each equation and check your answers.

a. $2x + 3 = 9$
b. $\frac{1}{2}x + 3 = 9$
c. $x + 3 = \frac{9}{2}$
d. $x + \frac{1}{2} = 9$
e. $\frac{x + 3}{2} = 9$

38. Use properties of equality and numbers to solve each equation for x. Check your answers.

a. $3 + 6x = 4x + 9$
b. $6x + 3 = 4x + 9$
c. $6x - 3 = 4x + 9$
d. $3 - 6x = 4x + 9$

39. Use the graph to answer each question.

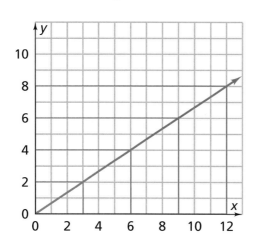

a. Are any of the rectangles in the picture above similar? If so, which rectangles, and explain why they are similar.

b. Find the slope of the diagonal line. How is it related to the similar rectangles?

c. Which of these rectangles belong to the set of rectangles in the graph? Explain.

40. The graph below shows the height of a rocket from 10 seconds before liftoff through 7 seconds after liftoff.

a. Describe the relationship between the height of the rocket and time.

b. What is the slope for the part of the graph that is a straight line? What does this slope represent in this situation?

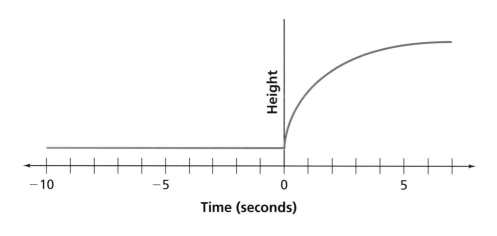

41. Solve each equation. Check your answers.

    a. $2(x + 5) = 18$ **b.** $2(x + 5) = x - 8$

    c. $2(x + 5) = x$ **d.** $2(x + 5) = -15$

42. Multiple Choice Which equation has a graph that contains the point $(-1, 6)$?

    A. $y = 4x + 1$ **B.** $y = -x + 5$ **C.** $y = 3x - 11$ **D.** $y = -3x + 11$

43. Each pair of figures is similar. Find the lengths of the sides marked x.

    a.

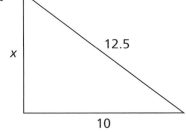

    b.

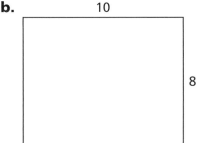

44. Find a value of n that will make each statement true.

    a. $\dfrac{n}{10} = \dfrac{3}{2}$ **b.** $\dfrac{5}{6} = \dfrac{n}{18}$ **c.** $-\dfrac{4}{6} = \dfrac{n}{3}$ **d.** $\dfrac{5}{18} = \dfrac{20}{n}$

    e. Write an equation for a line whose slope is $-\dfrac{4}{6}$.

45. Find a value of n that will make each statement true.

    a. $15\%(90) = n$ **b.** $20\%(n) = 80$ **c.** $n\%(50) = 5$

Extensions

46. On a March flight from Boston to Detroit, a monitor displayed the altitude and the outside air temperature. Two passengers that were on that flight tried to find a formula for temperature t in degrees Fahrenheit at an altitude of a feet above sea level. One passenger said the formula was $t = 46 - 0.003a$, and the other said it was $t = 46 + 0.003a$.

a. Which formula makes more sense to you? Why?

b. The Detroit Metropolitan Airport is 620 feet above sea level. Use the formula you chose in part (a) to find the temperature at the airport on that day.

c. Does the temperature you found in part (b) seem reasonable? Why or why not?

47. Andy's track team decides to convert their running rates from miles per hour to kilometers per hour (1 mile ≈ 1.6 kilometers).

a. Which method would you use to help the team do their converting: graph, table, or equation? Explain why you chose your method.

b. One of Andy's teammates said that he could write an equation for his spreadsheet program that could convert any team member's running rate from miles per hour to kilometers per hour. Write an equation that each member could use for this conversion.

Mathematical Reflections 4

In this investigation, you learned about the slope, or steepness, of a line. You learned how slope is related to an equation of the line and to a table or a graph of the equation. These questions will help you summarize what you have learned.

Think about your answers to these questions. Discuss your ideas with other students and your teacher. Then, write a summary of your findings in your notebook.

1. Explain what the slope of a line is. How does finding slope compare to finding the rate of change between two variables in a linear relationship?

2. How can you find the slope of a line from
   a. an equation?
   b. a graph?
   c. a table of values of the line?
   d. the coordinates of two points on the line?

3. For parts (a) and (b), explain how you can write an equation of a line from the information. Use examples to illustrate your thinking.
   a. the slope and the *y*-intercept of the line
   b. two points on the line

Unit Project

Conducting an Experiment

In many situations, patterns become apparent only after sufficient data are collected, organized, and displayed. Your group will be carrying out one of these experiments.

- In Project 1, you will investigate the rate at which a leaking faucet loses water.

- In Project 2, you will investigate how the drop height of a ball is related to its bounce height.

You will examine and use the patterns in the data collected from these experiments to make predictions.

Project 1: Wasted Water Experiment

In this experiment, you will simulate a leaking faucet and collect data about the volume of water lost at 5-second intervals. You will then use the patterns in your results to predict how much water is wasted when a faucet leaks for one month. Read the directions carefully before you start. Be prepared to explain your findings to the rest of the class.

Materials:

a styrofoam or paper cup

water

a paper clip

a clear measuring container (such as a graduated cylinder)

a watch or clock with a second hand

Directions:

Divide the work among the members of your group.

1. Make a table with columns for recording time and the amount of water lost. Fill in the time column with values from 0 seconds to 60 seconds in 5-second intervals (that is, 5, 10, 15, and so on).

2. Use the paper clip to punch a hole in the bottom of the paper cup. Cover the hole with your finger.

3. Fill the cup with water.

4. Hold the paper cup over the measuring container.

5. When you are ready to begin timing, uncover the hole so that the water drips into the measuring container, simulating the leaky faucet.

6. Record the amount of water in the measuring container at 5-second intervals for a minute.

Use this experiment to write an article for your local paper, trying to convince the people in your town to conserve water and fix leaky faucets. In your article, include the following information:

- a coordinate graph of the data you collected

- a description of the variables you investigated in this experiment and a description of the relationship between the variables

- a list showing your predictions for:

  - the amount of water that would be wasted in 15 seconds, 2 minutes, in 2.5 minutes, and in 3 minutes if a faucet dripped at the same rate as your cup does

  - how long it would it take for the container to overflow if a faucet dripped into the measuring container at the same rate as your cup

  Explain how you made your predictions. Did you use the table, the graph, or some other method? What clues in the data helped you?

- a description of other variables, besides time, that affect the amount of water in the measuring container

- a description of how much water would be wasted in one month if a faucet leaked at the same rate as your paper cup. Explain how you made your predictions

- the cost of the water wasted by a leaking faucet in one month (To do this, you will need to find out how much water costs in your area. Then, use this information to figure out the cost of the wasted water.)

Project 2: Ball Bounce Experiment

In this experiment, you will investigate how the height from which a ball is dropped is related to the height it bounces. Read the directions carefully before you start. Be prepared to explain your findings to the rest of the class.

Materials:

a meter stick

a ball that bounces

Directions:

Divide the work among the members of your group.

1. Make a table with columns for recording drop height and bounce height.

2. Hold the meter stick perpendicular to a flat surface, such as an uncarpeted floor, a table, or a desk.

3. Choose and record a height on the meter stick as the height from which you will drop the ball. Hold the ball so that either the top of the ball or the bottom of the ball is at this height.

4. Drop the ball and record the height of the first bounce. If the *top* of the ball was at your starting height, look for the height of the *top* of the ball. If the *bottom* of the ball was at your starting height, look for the height of the *bottom* of the ball. (You may have to do this several times before you feel confident you have a good estimate of the bounce height.)

5. Repeat this for several different starting heights.

After you have done completed the experiment, write a report that includes the following:

- a coordinate graph of the data you collected

- a description of the variables you investigated in this experiment and a description of the relationship between the variables

- a list showing your predictions for
  (a) the bounce height for a drop height of 2 meters
  (b) the drop height needed for a bounce height of 2 meters

- a description of how you made your prediction, whether you used a table, a graph, or some other method, and the clues in the data that helped you make your predictions

- an explanation of the bounce height you would expect for a drop height of 0 centimeters and where you could find this on the graph

- a description of any other variables besides the drop height, which may affect the bounce height of the ball

Looking Back and Looking Ahead

Unit Review

In the problems of this unit, you explored many examples of *linear relationships* between variables. You learned how to recognize linear patterns in *graphs* and in *tables* of numerical data and how to express those patterns in words and in symbolic *equations* or *formulas*. Most importantly, you learned how to study tables, graphs, and equations to answer questions about linear relationships.

For: Vocabulary Review
Puzzle
Web Code: anj-5051

Use Your Understanding: Algebraic Reasoning

Test your understanding of linear relationships by solving the following problems about the operation of a movie theater.

1. Suppose that a theater charges a school group $4.50 per student to show a special film. Suppose that the theater's operating expenses include $130 for the staff and a film rental fee of $1.25 per student.

    a. What equation relates the number of students x to the theater's income I?

    b. What equation relates the theater's operating expenses E to x?

    c. Copy and complete the table below.

Theater Income and Expenses

Number of Students, x	0	10	20	30	40	50	60	70
Income, I ($)	■	■	■	■	■	■	■	■
Expenses, E ($)	■	■	■	■	■	■	■	■

    d. On the same set of axes, graph the theater's income and operating expenses for any number of students from 0 to 100.

    e. Describe the patterns by which income and operating increase as the number of students increases.

    f. Write and solve an equation whose solution will answer the question "How many students need to attend the movie so that the theater's income will equal its operating expenses?"

2. At another theater, the income and expenses combine to give the equation $y = 3x - 115$ relating operating profit y to the number of students in a group x.

a. What do the numbers 3 and -115 tell about

   i. the relation between the number of students in a group and the theater's profit?

   ii. the pattern of entries that would appear in a table of sample (*students, profit*) pairs?

   iii. a graph of the relation between the number of students and the profit?

b. Use the equation to find the number of students necessary for the theater to

   i. break even (make 0 profit).

   ii. make a profit of $100.

c. Write and solve an equation that will find the number of students for which the theaters in Problem 1 and Problem 2 will make the same profit. Then find the amount of that profit.

Explain Your Reasoning

When you use mathematical calculations to solve a problem or make a decision, it is important to be able to justify each step in your reasoning. For Problems 1 and 2:

3. Consider the variables and relationships.

a. What are the variables?

b. Which pairs of variables are related to each other?

c. In each pair of related variables, how does change in the value of one variable cause change in the value of the other?

4. Which relationships are linear and which are not? What patterns in the tables, graphs, and symbolic equations support your conclusions?

5. For those relationships that are linear, what do the slopes and intercepts of the graphs indicate about the relationships involved?

6. How do the slopes and intercepts relate to data patterns in the various tables of values?

7. Consider the strategies for solving linear equations such as those in Problem 1, part (f), and Problem 2, part (c).

   a. How can the equations be solved using tables of values?

   b. How can you solve those equations by using graphs?

   c. How can you solve the equations by reasoning about the equations alone?

8. Suppose you were asked to write a report describing the relationships among number of students, theater income, and operating costs. What value might be gained by including the table? Including the graph? Including the equation? What are the limitations of each type of display?

Look Ahead

Examples of linear relationships and equations arise in many situations, but there are also important nonlinear relationships such as inverse, exponential, and quadratic. The algebraic ideas and techniques you've used in this unit are useful in problems of science and business. They will be applied and extended to other relationships in future units of Connected Mathematics such as *Thinking With Mathematical Models* and *Say It With Symbols*.

C

coefficient A number that is multiplied by a variable in an equation or expression. In a linear equation of the form $y = mx + b$, the number m is the coefficient of x as well as the slope of the line. For example, in the equation $y = 3x + 5$, the coefficient of x is 3. This is also the slope of the line.

coeficiente Un número que se multiplica por una variable en una ecuación o expresión. En una ecuación de la forma $y = mx + b$, el número m es el coeficiente de x y la inclinación de la recta. Por ejemplo, en la ecuación $y = 3x + 5$, el coeficiente de x es 3. También representa la pendiente de la recta.

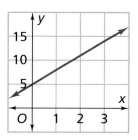

constant term A number in an equation that is not multiplied by a variable, or an amount added to or subtracted from the terms involving variables. In an equation of the form $y = mx + b$, the y-intercept, b, is a constant term. The effect of the constant term on a graph is to raise or lower the graph. The constant term in the equation $y = 3x + 5$ is 5. The graph of $y = 3x$ is raised vertically 5 units to give the graph of $y = 3x + 5$.

término constante Un número en una ecuación que no se multiplica por una variable, o una cantidad sumada o restada a los términos que contienen variables. En una ecuación de la forma $y = mx + b$, el punto de intersección de y, b, es un término constante. El término constante hace que la gráfica suba o baje. El término constante en la ecuación $y = 3x + 5$ es 5. Para obtener la gráfica de $y = 3x + 5$, la gráfica $y = 3x$ se sube 5 unidades sobre el eje vertical.

coordinate pair A pair of numbers of the form (x, y) that gives the location of a point in the coordinate plane. The x term gives the distance left or right from the origin $(0, 0)$, and the y term gives the distance up or down from the origin.

par de coordenadas Un par de números con la forma (x, y) que determina la ubicación de un punto en el plano de las coordenadas. El término x determina la distancia hacia la derecha o izquierda desde el punto de origen $(0, 0)$, y el término y determina la distancia hacia arriba o abajo desde el punto de origen.

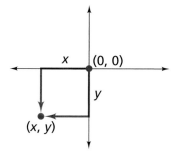

function A relationship between two variables in which the value of one variable depends on the value of the other variable. For example, the distance *d* in miles covered in *t* hours by a car traveling at 55 mph is given by the equation $d = 55t$. The relationship between distance and the time is a function, and we say that the distance is a *function* of the time. This function is a *linear function*, and its graph is a straight line whose slope is 55. In future units, you will learn about functions that are not linear.

función Una relación entre dos variables en la que el valor de una variable depende del valor de la otra. Por ejemplo, la distancia, *d*, recorrida en un número de *t* horas por un automóvil que viaja a 55 mph está representada por la ecuación $d = 55t$. La relación entre la distancia y el tiempo es una función, y decimos que la distancia es una *función* del tiempo. Esta función es una *función lineal* y se representa gráficamente como una línea recta con una pendiente de 55. En las próximas unidades vas a estudiar relaciones que no son lineales.

intersecting lines Lines that cross or *intersect*. The coordinates of the point where the lines intersect are solutions to the equations for both lines. The graphs of the equations $y = x$ and $y = 2x - 3$ intersect at the point (3, 3). This number pair is a solution to each equation.

rectas secantes Rectas que se cruzan o *intersectan*. Las coordenadas del punto del punto de intersección de las rectas son la solución de las ecuaciones de las dos rectas. Las gráficas de las ecuaciones $y = x$ e $y = 2x - 3$ se cortan en el punto (3, 3). Este par de números es la solución de las dos ecuaciones.

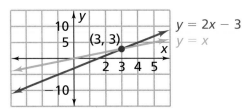

linear function See *function*.

función lineal Ver función.

linear relationship A relationship in which there is a constant rate of change between two variables; for each unit increase in one variable, there is a constant change in the other variable. For example, as *x* changes by a constant amount, *y* changes by a constant amount. A linear relationship between two variables can be represented by a straight-line graph and by an equation of the form $y = mx + b$. The rate of change is *m*, the coefficient of *x*. For example, if you save $2 each month, the relationship between the amount you save and the number of months is a linear relationship that can be represented by the equation $y = 2x$. The constant rate of change is 2.

relación lineal Una relación en la que hay una tasa de variación constante entre dos variables; por cada unidad que aumenta una variable, hay una variación constante en la otra variable. Por ejemplo, a medida que *x* cambia una cantidad constante, *y* cambia en una cantidad constante. Una relación lineal entre dos variables puede representarse con una gráfica de línea recta y con una ecuación de la forma $y = mx + b$. La tasa de variación es *m*, el coeficiente de *x*. Por ejemplo, si ahorras $2 por mes, la relación entre la cantidad que ahorras por mes y el número de meses es una relación lineal que puede representarse con la ecuación $y = 2x$. La tasa de variación constante es 2.

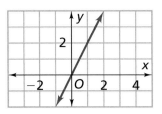

origin The point where the x- and y-axes intersect on a coordinate graph. With coordinates $(0, 0)$, the origin is the center of the coordinate plane.

origen El punto en que los ejes de las x y las y se cortan en una gráfica de coordenadas. Si las coordenadas son $(0, 0)$, el origen se halla en el centro del plano de las coordenadas.

point of intersection The point where two lines intersect. If the lines are represented on a coordinate grid, the coordinates for the point of intersection can be read from the graph.

punto de intersección El punto donde dos rectas se intersecan. Si las rectas están representadas en una cuadrícula de coordenadas, las coordenadas del punto de intersección se pueden leer de la gráfica.

properties of equality For all real numbers, a, b, and c:

　Addition: If $a = b$, then $a + c = b + c$.
　Subtraction: If $a = b$, then $a - c = b - c$.
　Multiplication: If $a = b$, then $a \cdot c = b \cdot c$.
　Division: If $a = b$, and $c \neq 0$, then $\frac{a}{c} = \frac{b}{c}$.

propiedades de una igualdad Para todos los números reales a, b, y c:

　Suma: Si $a = b$, entonces $a + c = b + c$.
　Resta: Si $a = b$, entonces $a - c = b - c$.
　Multiplicación: Si $a = b$, entonces $a \cdot c = b \cdot c$.
　División: Si $a = b$, y $c \neq 0$, entonces $\frac{a}{c} = \frac{b}{c}$.

rise The vertical change between two points on a graph. The slope of a line is the rise divided by the run.

alzada La variación vertical entre dos puntos en la gráfica. La inclinación de una recta es la alzada dividida por la huella.

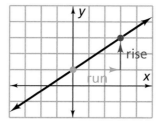

run The horizontal change between two points on a graph. The slope of a line is the rise divided by the run.

huella La variación horizontal entre dos puntos en la gráfica. La pendiente de una recta es la alzada dividida por la huella.

scale The distance between two consecutive tick marks on the x- and y-axes of a coordinate grid. When graphing, an appropriate scale must be selected so that the resulting graph will be clearly shown. For example, when graphing the equation $y = 60x$, a scale of 1 for the x-axis and a scale of 15 or 30 for the y-axis would be reasonable.

escala La distancia entre dos marcas consecutivas en los ejes x e y de una cuadrícula de coordenadas. Cuando se realiza una gráfica, se debe seleccionar una escala apropiada de manera que represente con claridad la gráfica resultante. Por ejemplo, para la representación gráfica de la ecuación $y = 60x$, una escala razonable resultaría 1 para el eje de x y una escala de 15 ó 30 para el eje de y.

slope The number that expresses the steepness of a line. The slope is the ratio of the vertical change to the horizontal change between any two points on the line. Sometimes this ratio is referred to as *the rise over the run*. The slope of a horizontal line is 0. Slopes are positive if the y-values increase from left to right on a coordinate grid and negative if the y-values decrease from left to right. The slope of a vertical line is undefined. The slope of a line is the same as the constant rate of change between the two variables. For example, the points $(0, 0)$ and $(3, 6)$ lie on the graph of $y = 2x$. Between these points, the vertical change is 6 and the horizontal change is 3, so the slope is $\frac{6}{3} = 2$, which is the coefficient of x in the equation.

pendiente El número que expresa la inclinación de una recta. La pendiente es la razón entre la variación vertical y la horizontal entre dos puntos cualesquiera de la recta. A veces a esta razón se *la denomina alzada sobre huella*. La pendiente de una recta horizontal es 0. Las pendientes son positivas si los valores de y aumentan de izquierda a derecha en una cuadrícula de coordenadas, y negativas si los valores de y decrecen de izquierda a derecha. La pendiente de una recta vertical es indefinida. La pendiente de una recta es igual a la tasa de variación constante entre dos variables. Por ejemplo, los puntos $(0, 0)$ y $(3, 6)$ están representados en la gráfica de $y = 2x$. Entre estos puntos, la variación vertical es 6 y la variación horizontal es 3, de manera que la pendiente es $\frac{6}{3} = 2$, que es el coeficiente de x en la ecuación.

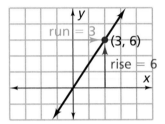

X

x-intercept The point where a graph crosses the x-axis. The x-intercept of the equation $y = 3x + 5$ is $\left(-\frac{5}{3}, 0\right)$ or $-\frac{5}{3}$.

punto de intersección de x El punto en el que la gráfica corta el eje de las x. El punto de intersección de x de la ecuación $y = 3x + 5$ es $\left(-\frac{5}{3}, 0\right)$ ó $-\frac{5}{3}$.

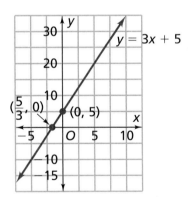

Y

y-intercept The point where the graph crosses the y-axis. In a linear equation of the form $y = mx + b$, the y-intercept is the constant, b. In the graph above, the y-intercept is $(0, 5)$, or 5.

punto de intersección de y El punto en el que la gráfica corta el eje de las y. En una ecuación lineal de la forma $y = mx + b$, el punto de intersección de y es la constante, b. En la gráfica anterior, el punto de intersección de y es $(0, 5)$ ó 5.

Index

Area model, 40–41, 63–64, 86–87

Break-even point, 56, 62

Calculator graph, 39

Check for reasonableness, 16–17, 29–30, 51, 53–54, 59, 61, 67, 85, 87–88

Coefficient, 27–28, 36, 65, 70–71, 76, 97, 99, 100

Comparing
  equations, 27–29, 53
  graphs, 9, 14–15, 22, 26, 31, 63, 75, 82–83, 94

Concrete model, *see* **Model**

Constant term, 97

Coordinate grid, making, 80, 85

Coordinate pair, 97

Dependent variable, 8–9, 15, 23

Diagram, 17, 43, 71–72, 78
  making, 71, 78

Distributive Property, 40–41

Equality, 48–54, 59–60
  properties of, 53–54, 59, 85, 99

Equation, *see* **Linear equation**

Experiment
  bouncing balls, 92–93
  calculating steepness, 71
  leak rate, 90–91
  walking rate, 6

Function (*see also*** Linear relationship),** 98

General form, of a linear equation, 27, 45, 70, 97–98, 100

Glossary, 97–100

Graph, *see* **Linear graph**

Independent variable, 8–9, 15, 23

Interpreting data
  area model, 40–41, 63–64, 86–87
  calculator graph, 39
  coordinate grid, 80, 85
  diagram, 17, 43, 71–72, 78

graph, 5–7, 9, 11–23, 26–27, 29–30, 32–35, 37–40, 43–46, 48, 54–55, 57, 60–63, 65, 68–71, 73–75, 78, 81–83, 86–87, 89, 91, 93–94, 96–100
  picture, 31, 50–52, 58, 61
  table, 5–7, 9–13, 15–16, 18–21, 23, 26, 29–30, 34–35, 41, 43, 45, 47–48, 54, 57, 60–61, 68–69, 73–74, 79–82, 89, 90–92, 94, 96

Intersecting line, 98

Investigations
  Exploring Linear Functions With Graphs and Tables, 24–45
  Exploring Slope, 70–89
  Solving Equations, 46–69
  Walking Rates, 5–23

Justify answer, 7–8, 10–11, 25–26, 28–30, 48, 50–51, 53–56, 73–75, 77, 89, 91, 93, 95–96
  ACE, 12, 15, 19–20, 22, 31, 34–35, 37, 39–44, 57–63, 66–68, 80, 82, 84–86, 88

Justify method, 11, 25, 29–30, 45, 48, 51, 53–56, 69, 73–75, 77, 89, 91, 93, 96
  ACE, 13, 21, 34–35, 57, 60, 63, 68, 88

Linear equation, 4–96
  ACE, 12–22, 31–44, 57–68, 78–88
  checking solutions, 16–17, 29, 51, 53–54, 59, 67, 85, 87
  comparing, 27–29, 53
  and equality, 48–54, 59–60
  general form of, 27, 45, 70, 97–98, 100
  rate and, 5–23
  solving, 46–69
  with two variables, 76–77
  writing, 6–7, 9–18, 26, 31, 34–38, 40–42, 44, 51–52, 58, 63, 65–68, 71, 74–78, 81–85, 87–88, 94–95

Linear function, *see* **Linear relationship**

Linear graph, 5–7, 9, 11, 23, 26–27, 29–30, 45–46, 48, 54–55, 69–71, 73–75, 89, 91, 93–94, 96–100
  ACE, 12–22, 32–35, 37–40, 43–44, 57, 60–63, 65, 68, 78, 81–83, 86–87
  comparing, 9, 14–15, 22, 26, 31, 63, 75, 82–83, 94
  making, 7, 9, 12–13, 15, 18, 21–22, 26, 30, 37, 44, 63, 65, 68, 71, 75, 78, 82, 91, 93
  rate and, 5–7, 9, 11–23

Linear relationship, 4–96, 98
  ACE, 12–22, 31–44, 57–68, 78–88
  definition, 5, 99
  rate and, 5–23
  slope and, 70–89
  writing an equation for, *see* Linear equation

Looking Back and Looking Ahead: Unit Review, 94–96

Manipulatives
  experimental equipment, 6, 71, 90–93

Mathematical Highlights, 4

Mathematical Reflections, 23, 45, 69, 89

Model
  area, 40–41, 63–64, 86–87
  calculator graph, 39
  diagram, 17, 43, 71–72
  graph, 5, 11, 14, 16, 19–21, 27, 29, 32–33, 38–40, 43, 46, 55, 73–74, 78, 81–83, 86, 97–100
  picture, 31, 50–52, 58, 61

Negative reciprocal, 84

Negative slope, 72–73, 79, 100

Notebook, 23, 45, 69, 89

Organized list, making, 91, 93

Origin, 99

Pattern, 4
  looking for a, 9, 15–16, 20, 23, 35, 45, 75, 90–96
  and slope, 75, 96

Index

Pictorial model, *see* **Model**

Picture, 31, 50–52, 58, 61
  drawing, 58

Point of intersection (*see also***
    y-intercept),** 32, 55–56, 63,
    99

Positive slope, 72–73, 79, 81, 100

Problem-solving strategies
  drawing a picture, 58
  looking for a pattern, 9, 15–16,
    20, 23, 35, 45, 75, 90–96
  making a coordinate grid, 80,
    85
  making a diagram, 71, 78
  making a graph, 7, 9, 12–13, 15,
    18, 21–22, 26, 30, 37, 44, 63,
    65, 68, 71, 75, 78, 82, 91, 93
  making an organized list, 91, 93
  making a table, 7, 9, 11, 19, 26,
    30, 41, 43, 68, 73–74, 80, 82,
    90, 92, 94
  writing an equation, 6–7, 9–18,
    26, 31, 34–38, 40–42, 44,
    51–52, 58, 63, 65–68, 71,
    74–78, 81–85, 87–88, 94–95

Properties of equality, 53–54, 59,
    85, 99

Rate, 5–23
  ACE, 12–22
  linear relationship and, 5–23

Rate of change, *see* **Rate**

Ratio, for slope, 71–72, 100

Rise, steepness and, 71–72, 78,
    99–100

Run, steepness and, 71–72, 78,
    99–100

Scale, 99

Slope, 70–89, 96, 97–99
  ACE, 78–88
  definition, 72, 100
  finding, 72–74
  negative, 72–73, 79, 100
  and patterns, 75, 96
  positive, 72–73, 79, 81, 100
  ratio for, 71–72, 100
  tables and, 73–74, 79–82, 89, 96
  undefined, 100

Steepness (*see also* **Slope),**
    70–72, 85, 89, 100

Table, 5–7, 9–11, 23, 26, 29–30,
    45, 47–48, 54, 69, 73–74, 89,
    90–92, 94, 96
  ACE, 12–13, 15–16, 18–21,
    34–35, 41, 43, 57, 60–61, 68,
    79–82
  making, 7, 9, 11, 19, 26, 30, 41,
    43, 68, 73–74, 80, 82, 90, 92,
    94
  rate and, 5–7, 9–13, 15–16,
    18–21, 23
  slope and, 73–74, 79–82, 89, 96

Undefined slope, 100

**Unit Project: Conducting an
    Experiment,** 90–93

Variables, 4, 5, 8–9, 11, 23, 47–48,
    51–54, 91, 93, 95, 98
  ACE, 15–16, 43, 57–58, 67
  dependent, 8–9, 15, 23
  independent, 8–9, 15, 23

x-intercept, 40, 61, 80, 96, 100

y-intercept, 27–28, 56, 74, 76–77,
    89, 96–97, 100
  ACE, 36–37, 40, 61, 65, 79–80,
    84

Acknowledgments

Team Credits

The people who made up the **Connected Mathematics 2** team—representing editorial, editorial services, design services, and production services—are listed below. Bold type denotes core team members.

Leora Adler, Judith Buice, Kerry Cashman, Patrick Culleton, Sheila DeFazio, Richard Heater, **Barbara Hollingdale, Jayne Holman,** Karen Holtzman, **Etta Jacobs,** Christine Lee, Carolyn Lock, Catherine Maglio, **Dotti Marshall,** Rich McMahon, Eve Melnechuk, Kristin Mingrone, Terri Mitchell, **Marsha Novak,** Irene Rubin, Donna Russo, Robin Samper, Siri Schwartzman, **Nancy Smith,** Emily Soltanoff, **Mark Tricca,** Paula Vergith, Roberta Warshaw, Helen Young

Additional Credits

Diana Bonfilio, Mairead Reddin, Michael Torocsik, nSight, Inc.

Technical Illustration

WestWords, Inc.

Cover Design

tom white.images

Photos

2 t, Joe Carini/The Image Works; **2 b,** David Young-Wolff/Alamy; **3,** Zoran Milich/Masterfile; **11,** Siri Schwartzman; **13,** David Stoecklein/ Corbis; **18,** Martin Bureau/AFP/Getty Images, Inc.; **22,** Blasius Erlinger/Getty Images, Inc.; **24,** Mark Leibowitz/Masterfile; **25,** Joe Carini/ The Image Works; **26,** Michael Steele/Getty Images, Inc.; **28,** Don Tremain/Getty Images, Inc.; **32,** David Young-Wolff/Photo Edit; **33,** Robert W. Ginn/PhotoEdit; **34,** AP Photo/The Paris News, Bill Ridder; **36,** Andrew Olney/Masterfile; **42,** Larry Williams/Corbis; **47,** Richard Haynes; **53,** Richard Haynes; **56,** AP Photo/The Plain Dealer, Chris Stephens; **62,** Royalty-Free/Corbis; **66,** Michael Newman/Photo Edit; **68,** Mike Dembeck/AFP/Getty Images, Inc.; **70,** Russ Schleipman/Index Stock Imagery, Inc.; **73,** Richard Haynes; **76,** David Young-Wolff/ Alamy; **78,** OnRequest Images, Inc./Alamy; **85 l,** Powered by Light/Alan Spencer/Alamy; **85 r,** Ian Connellan/Lonely Planet Images; **88,** Bob Daemmrich/The Image Works; **93,** Royalty-Free/Corbis

Acknowledgments